MULL AND IONA

P. A. MACNAB

David & Charles
Newton Abbot   London   North Pomfret (Vt)

British Library Cataloguing in Publication Data

Macnab, P. A.
  Mull and Iona. – 2nd rev. ed. – (The Island
series)
  1. Iona (Scotland) – Description and travel
  – Guide-books   2. Mull, Island of (Scotland)
  – Description and travel – Guide-books
  I. Title   II. Series
  914.14′23   DA880.I7

  ISBN 0-7153-8901-7

First published as *The Isle of Mull 1970*
Reprinted 1973
Second revised edition 1987

Phototypeset by Typesetters (Birmingham) Ltd,
Smethwick, West Midlands
and printed in Great Britain
by Redwood Burn Ltd, Trowbridge
for David & Charles Publishers plc
Brunel House   Newton Abbot   Devon

Published in the United States of America
by David & Charles Inc
North Pomfret   Vermont 05053   USA

To my forefathers
and the people of Mull

CONTENTS

ILLUSTRATIONS

8

Photographs other than those acknowledged are by the author

IN TEXT

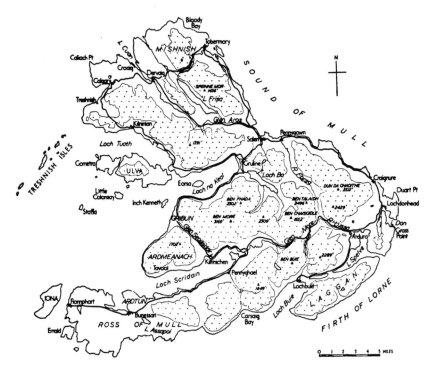

The Isle of Mull
Land over 500ft is shown stippled

INTRODUCTION

THE anthem of Mull, *An t'eilean Muileach*, a popular
Gaelic song composed by the Mull bard Dugald
MacPhail, is a fittingly descriptive introduction to this
island of contrasts. In English it runs:

> The Isle of Mull is of isles the fairest,
> Of ocean's gems 'tis the first and rarest
> Green grassy island of sparkling fountains,
> Of waving woods and high tow'ring mountains.

For the island is a place of high hills and bare moorlands, yet
with lush growth and tall trees in sheltered glens, or with
stunted shrubs grasping a precarious living along the wind-
swept and spray-battered cliffs which face the western ocean.
Although its coasts are rocky and heavily indented with bays
and sea-lochs, in the south-west there are fine sandy beaches
backed by green machair lands and little crofting communities. In the north-west one comes unexpectedly upon a few
beaches of dazzling white shell sand separated by cliffs of dark
basalt.

However, although Mull is regarded as a typical Hebridean
island, beset by the economic and social problems common to
the Scottish Highlands and Islands, it has certain unique
characteristics which will emerge later in this book. While
other islands have their individual features – scenic beauty,
geological structure, social history, botany, etc – in Mull,
centrally and conveniently situated as it is in relation to the
mainland, all these features are present, and in addition
others found nowhere else in the Hebridean islands. Unlike
other mountainous islands of the Hebrides all but the highest
and most rugged of its hills have a green pastoral beauty, with
rich grazings extending far up to the summit ridges. The
attractions of the island were certainly missed by Dr Johnson

during his visit with Boswell on a drab, wet October day in 1773. The learned doctor described it as 'Mull, a dreary country, much worse than Sky [Skye] . . . a most dolorous country'. Boswell, slightly more discerning, disagreed: 'a hilly country . . . diversified with heath and grass, and many rivulets'.

Mull has a character all of its own. For instance, the many ruined pre-Reformation chapels scattered through the island – there are at least fourteen of them – are evidence that Mull shared the ecclesiastical radiance emanating from the little island of Iona, off its south-west corner.

Mull is also distinguished by the fact that it is commemorated on the maps of Britain's former colonies and dominions more generously than any other part of the British Isles – with such names as Glengorm, Tobermory, Glenmore, Glenforsa, Inch Kenneth, Knock, Ulva, Kilmore, MacLaine Plains, and many others – especially in Australia, where Maj-Gen Lachlan Macquarie during his governorship thirled the new continent firmly to his beloved native island by a selection of nostalgic place names. Calgary, Alberta, was so named when Col J. F. Macleod, a native of Skye, Commander of the Royal North-West Mounted Police in Canada, was setting up a new post and township. Seeking a name for it, his thoughts turned to happy visits he had paid to Calgary House in Mull. (The name was not, as is popularly supposed, bestowed by emigrants from Calgary who had to leave during the Clearances.) The name Calgary, by the way, comes either from *Cala(g)airidh*, the harbour of the sheilings, or – more probably – *Cala a'Gharaidh*, the harbour, or haven, by the wall.

Mull – *Malaeius* – is one of the five islands lying north of Ireland mentioned by Ptolemy known collectively as the *Ebuda* – hence 'Hebrides'. When the Roman armies invaded Scotland they stopped short of the island's then inhospitable shores; but before them peoples of the Stone, Bronze and Iron Ages had settled in Mull, and like the later Celts from Ireland, the Christians and the Norsemen, warring clansmen and latter-day crofters, all left records behind them in the form of standing stones, forts, stone chapels, carvings, castles or habitations.

According to the census of 1821 Mull then supported a population of over 10,000. Reduced in number now to about 2,365, the people are scattered amongst isolated sheep-farms, agricultural units, forestry centres, and private houses where more and more retired people come to seek peace and privacy. Apart from the little town of Tobermory there are only a few centres of population and they house no more than 150 or 200 people at most. In the 1970s there was a marked increase in the building of holiday homes which are occupied for only part of the year.

In the south-west lies the hamlet of Fionnphort (approximate population 40), from which the little ferry-boat crosses the mile-wide Sound of Iona to the village there (122). A few miles inland, along the main road and standing at the head of a wide, sheltered sea-loch, lies Bunessan (100), a more pretentious little village; but beyond that there is no settlement of note, apart from the tiny hamlet of Pennyghael, until one reaches the east coast. There one comes to Lochdonhead (60), a single row of houses curving round a small shallow bay overlooked by high mountains. Further west, along the northeast coast on the Sound of Mull, lies Craignure (130), terminus for the car ferry from Oban and a settlement likely to grow, although land is difficult to acquire. Beyond this, halfway along the Sound of Mull, Salen (260) is a scattered village established at the beginning of the nineteenth century. This is a focal point for the road system of the island. Dervaig (150) in the north-west was established about the same time as Salen although by a different landowner and remains one of the most attractive villages in the Hebrides. In 1986 Dervaig village and part of the upper estuary were designated a Conservation Area. Everywhere in these settlements the older houses are uniformly austere in construction and design and they have steadily been brought up to modern standards.

The one real centre of population and the capital of the island is Tobermory. Its Gaelic name is *Tobar Mhoire*, Well of Mary, and it grew on a site where a small Christian settlement dedicated to St Mary had been founded in early times. The foundations of an old chapel can be seen to the left of the entrance gate of the old cemetery in the Upper Village, and

13

the well lies somewhere in the hollow behind the ornamental fountain built to commemorate the coronation of Edward VII, quite near the cemetery wall.

Tobermory was the smallest Burgh in Scotland, until its identity was lost in the reorganisation of local government in 1973, when its population was just over 600. That figure is slowly on the increase (843 in 1981). While its magnificent bay, the finest in the Hebrides, will always ensure a measure of importance, nevertheless the focus of shipping and transportation has moved to Craignure, 22 miles nearer Oban along the Sound of Mull, since the building of the new pier there in 1964 and its later conversion to roll-on roll-off for the highly convenient handling of motor cars by large car ferries. The town is more fully discussed in a later chapter.

Before moving on to a detailed survey of Mull, mention must be made of the vital part played by Tobermory as a naval base during World War II, a record too easily forgotten. It was a hive of activity well described in Richard Baker's book *The Terror of Tobermory* (W. H. Allen, 1972). Here, under the inspired and unorthodox training organised by Vice-Adml Sir Gilbert Stephenson, KBE, CB, CMG, ('The Terror'), nearly 1,000 newly commissioned escort ships up to destroyer size and about 250,000 men were welded into such highly efficient units in the remarkably short time of a fortnight that they accounted for an estimated total of no less than 130 enemy U-boats and 40 aircraft during the war. Well might Tobermory be described officially as '. . . the most disciplined, orderly and efficient base in the British Isles' and 'the cradle of victory in the Atlantic'.

The redoubtable admiral (known familiarly as 'Puggy', 'Monkey' or 'Monkey Brand'), whose base was HMS *Western Isles*, a converted passenger vessel formerly on the Liverpool to Isle of Man run, was knighted in 1943 for his immense contribution to the war effort.

LANDSCAPES

Mull is the third largest island in the Hebrides, exceeded in area only by Lewis and Skye. It covers about 225,000 acres

(90,000ha) and is roughly 24 miles from north to south and 26 miles from east to west. These figures, however, give no indication of the length of its coastline, which is so broken by long sea-lochs and bays and inlets that it is over 300 miles long. By road from Tobermory to Fionnphort (for Iona) it is 50 miles. The island has been separated from the mainland by the breaching of the peninsula, of which it must have been a part, by what is now the Sound of Mull, a sheltered waterway about 35 miles long and varying in width from 5 miles to less than 2 miles. North of these waters lie the mainland peninsulas of Morvern and Ardnamurchan. On the east the island is washed by the waters of Loch Linnhe and its south-westerly projection, the Firth of Lorne; east of these channels lies the mainland of Argyll. Facing the eastern end of Mull and less than 10 miles distant is the busy town of Oban, the main point of communications between the island and the mainland.

Mull is famed in song and story as 'Mull of the Mountains'. Its peaks are landmarks in the whole of the southern Hebrides and from distant hills of the mainland. Despite their height, however, the hills of Mull are more rounded, gentler, as it were, than the rugged hills of Skye, or Rhum, or the mainland hills; and provided that common sense is used their exploration is comparatively easy and safe. The highest peak, Ben More ('The Big Hill'), at 3,169ft (966m) above sea-level, is the only 'Munro' in the Hebrides outside the Cuillin Hills in Skye. (A 'Munro' is a hill of 3,000ft/915m or more, isolated by a dip of at least 500ft/152m, called after the Scottish mountaineer who first listed such peaks.) The ascent, either from Loch na Keal to the north, or from Loch Scridain to the south, need be no more than a few hours' hard hill walking. Of course it can be chilly at the top. Ascending from sea-level, about 1°F of temperature is lost for every 300ft (90m) of elevation.

The most arresting views in Mull lie around Loch na Keal and Loch Tuath and the most advantageous viewpoints are from Torloisk, on the north side, or where the road climbs above Gribun on the south side. The panorama of the Ben More peaks runs westwards into the high headlands of Gribun and Ardmeanach, where the horizontal lava flows – one of the

15

island's most typical and spectacular aspects of geology – end abruptly in high cliffs, for all the world resembling the silhouettes of the ram bows of old-time dreadnoughts. The cliffs are cleft by ravines and chimneys through which many burns pour, reminding the onlooker vividly of Tennyson's lines:

> And like a downward smoke, the slender stream
> Along the cliff to fall and pause and fall did seem.
> A land of streams . . .

Mull is indeed a land of streams – wherever you stand the sound of running water is seldom absent. When the gales blow in from the Atlantic, some waterfalls, such as Eas Fors at the east end of Loch Tuath, or Allt Airidh nan Chaisteal in Ardmeanach, are checked in their descent and blown back in spray over the cliff tops, until the whole headland appears to be smoking as if on fire. Diverted by the headlands, the gusts of wind also play mad tricks along the sea-lochs, creating violent eddies which draw up the waters into miniature water-spouts extending far out from the shore.

Beyond the western promontories of the main island, the Treshnish Islands fill the horizon with their strange outlines, like high-bowed ships sailing eternally into the south-west. Still further out lies the long, low rocky island of Coll and to the south-west of this the flat sandy line of Tiree – 'the island that is lower than the waves', as the old folk used to call it – where the weather station has recorded some of the highest wind velocities around the British coasts. Dimly, on the far horizon, the higher peaks of the Long Island, from Barra Head to Harris, are spaced out at the edge of the world, as it were, for the lower parts of the islands are hidden.

Hemmed in by reefs and headlands, the tides run strongly along the coasts. A choppy sea with dangerous tide-rips can develop off Caliach Point in the north-west and between Duart and Lismore at the island's eastern end; elsewhere around the coasts the reefs can be a danger to shipping, particularly the Torran ('Thunder') Rocks and skerries south of Iona so vividly described by Robert Louis Stevenson in *Kidnapped*.

1   THE STRUCTURE AND CLIMATE OF MULL

A memoir issued by the Geological Survey of Scotland in 1924 begins: 'It may safely be maintained that Mull includes the most complicated igneous centre as yet accorded detailed examination anywhere in the world.' The unravelling of the geological story of the island started over two hundred years ago.

The island of Mull is, to put it simply, a worn-down land surface composed of vast sheets of lava flows deeply covering an extension of the ancient Caledonian rocks of the adjacent mainland, of which Mull once formed a part. Those old rocks, formed by complex earth movements about 300 million years ago, were greatly eroded by the time the Tertiary Age set in about 60 million years ago. Mull then became one of the active volcanic centres that broke through the older rocks, which extended in a great curve from the Mountains of Mourne in Ireland across the Hebrides as far as Iceland and beyond. During the next 10 million years, as a result of intermittent volcanic outpourings, Mull became an area of piled-up lavas that stretched far beyond its present coast line, massively eroded, then glaciated during the later Ice Age, to form the present landscape.

The general direction of coasts, glens and lochs still conforms roughly to similar features on the western mainland, mostly running northeast to southwest following structural lines of weakness that occurred during the Caledonian earth movements. The line of the Great Glen, or Caledonian Fault, crossing Scotland from the Moray Firth, continues through Loch Linnhe and cuts across the southeastern corner of Mull through Loch Spelve and Lochbuie. Another major feature known as the Moine Thrust Plane extends south-south-westerly from just east of Cape Wrath, continuing under the sea until, as is thought, it passes through the Sound of Iona. Iona lies west of this line and differs geologically from Mull, just across the Sound, in that it consists largely of very ancient rocks, Lewisian Gneiss, of which the Outer Hebrides are also composed, estimated to be 1,500 million years old and among the oldest rocks in the world.

Mull can be divided into three areas, the central mountain core, the northwest extension, and the Ross of Mull, with a small area of lowland in the eastern corner between Craignure and Loch Spelve, following the depression of the Great Glen Fault. Here the overlying lavas have been worn away to expose a 'window', so to speak, into the older rocks of the mainland through an upfolding in the strata.

THE MOUNTAIN CORE

This is a spectacular region of high jutting mountains and deep glens associated with the complex volcanic centre at the head of Loch Ba. Apart from Ben More, the highest peaks rise to 2512ft (766m) at Dun da Ghaoithe (Hill of the Two Winds). It extends westwards into the bold 1800ft (550m) plateau above Gribun and on to the 1000ft (305m) cliffs of the headland of Ardmeanach. Ben More, on the western perimeter of the volcanic centre, is at 3169ft (966m) the highest peak of tertiary basalts in Britain with an estimated thickness of 3000ft (915m) of basalts. It has been eroded massively from a maximum elevation which may have been 7000 to 8000ft (2000 to 2500m) down to its present height. Looking across Loch Scridain from the south a viewer can trace the horizontal edges of successive lava flows along the steep hill slopes of the Ardmeanach peninsula.

Gribun is a specially interesting area for exploration by geologists, for along the shore and exposed in the lower cliffs there are outcrops of sedimentary rocks, some of them fossiliferous, a most unusual formation in Mull, exposed possibly as the result of uplift in the coastal zone when the central volcanics subsided.

Ben Chasgidale (1652ft, 497m) beside Glen Cannel, is the

eroded core of the great volcano from which, at the beginning of the Tertiary Age, a vast quantity of lava of a basic consistency (that is, free-flowing), hardening into fine-grained basalts, poured out and built up to great heights. Fissures and lesser vents elsewhere on the island added their quota of lava.

Intervals of thousands of years occurred between flows, sometimes long enough for the surface to weather, soil to gather, and vegetation to flourish until submerged by the next flow. Later in the Tertiary period further activity of a different volcanic nature began. The Ben Chasgidle volcano was replaced by a second and overlapping vent situated about a mile to the north, at the head of Loch Ba, now worn down level with the floor of the glen. This time the lava was of a

Geological sketch map

more viscous nature and was ejected explosively to form into coarse grained rocks such as granite and gabbro.

At the end of the Tertiary Age, about 50 million years ago, there was left an area of massive subsidences surrounded by a complexity of ring dykes (a dyke is, of course, a fissure in the rocks filled with lava under pressure from below), which has attracted geologists to unravel the story.

THE NORTH-WEST AREA

This region is almost severed from the central core by Loch na Keal (or Loch na Cille, the Loch of the Cells of Missionaries), which leaves an isthmus of only three miles across to Salen, on the Sound of Mull. Similarly, Loch Tuath (the North Loch) has cut into the west coast and isolated the island of Ulva at Ulva Ferry. The region consists of flat boggy moorland, rising to terraced uplands and isolated flat-topped hills ('mesas') of the trap country. This word comes from Swedish *Trappa*, a step, and indeed Mull is a text-book example of this type of scenery. The hills rise to no more than 1456ft (444m) in Speinne Mor, which rises above Mull's longest freshwater loch, Loch Frisa, four miles in length. There are bold headlands and cliffs along the northern and western coasts.

The suffix 'nish' appearing in place names in the north of Mull such as Mishnish, Quinish, and so on indicates an isolated flat plateau: the name 'Mull' implies a larger, high, wide tableland, descriptive terms best understood when the island is viewed from the sea.

About four miles west of Tobermory the flat-topped hill of 'S Airde Ben (959ft – 292m) is one of the later and smaller vents that broke through the earlier lavas and is composed of a plug of later volcanic materials eroded with a little loch on the summit.

Around Loch na Keal, the Sound of Mull, and other locations, raised beaches are a feature, especially the 25ft beach which is backed by old sea cliffs and caves. Those raised beaches were formed when the whole land surface was rising when relieved of its burden of ice at the end of the Ice Age, and the loss of heavy deposits of volcanic materials by erosion over the ages: for of course the surface of the earth is like an elastic cover over its molten interior.

THE ROSS OF MULL

The long flatish Ross of Mull is separated from central Mull by the isthmus between the head of Loch Scridain and Loch Buie. The eastern end is covered by lava flows to a height of 1500ft (455m). The surface slopes up from Loch Scridain to the high cliffs of the southern coast. West of Bunessan there is a low area of worn-down ancient crystalline rocks, and west of Loch Lathaich are the famous red and pink granites. There are some fine sandy beaches in the southwest.

The uniform stretch of high cliffs on the south coast are broken by the picturesque bay of Carsaig, with its amphitheatre of 700ft (215m) cliffs towering above green grassy fields above the shore of dark basalt sand, and Loch Buie, which is backed by a small fertile plain. Fossiliferous sedimentary deposits outcrop to the west of Carsaig Bay; but of even greater interest is the outcrop of lignitic coal on the slopes of the hill southwest of Carsaig. This deposit, which occurs between the lava sheets, indicates the existence at one time of sub-tropical conditions, with a growth of vegetation, during intervals between the laying down of successive lava beds.

Caves above the Carsaig shoreline are associated with a higher sea level, such as the Nuns' Cave at Carsaig, the Carsaig Arches, and Lord Lovat's Cave near Lochbuie.

More evidence of changing climatic conditions is to be found in the well-known 'leaf beds' of Ardtun, near Bunessan, an accumulation of fossil leaves and petals in a layer of mudstone lying between two early lava flows. How the leaves accumulated is reconstructed in a paper presented in 1851 to the Geological Society of London by the 8th Duke of Argyll. In his paper, the Duke described how the leaves must have been shed autumn after autumn into the still waters of a shallow lake, on whose muddy bottom they accumulated in layers, fully expanded and at perfect rest. Botanical examination of the leaf beds, in the thin plates into which the mudstone can be split, showed that the leaves were from trees now found in sub-tropical conditions, ginko, sequoia and various conifers.

COLUMNAR BASALT

Nowhere else in Britain are such spectacular and well-known examples of columnar basalt found. This formation is limited to the earliest lava flows, and also, to judge from the distribution, to a limited area towards the west. The best examples are seen on the island of Staffa (Pillar Island); at the base of the Ulva basalts; in the Wilderness area of Ardmeanach; around the leaf beds at Ardtun, and in the Carsaig cliffs and Arches. Rudimentary columnar forms occur in most parts of the island.

Columnar formations were formed by cooling and contracting. The lava sheets began to cool with the upper faces losing heat most rapidly, the base more slowly and regularly. This led to the development of regular jointing at right angles to the cooling surfaces, and the resultant columns are usually hexagonal, although sometimes with between three and eight sides. This conforms to Nature's rule on economising space: for example, if a bundle of cigarettes is squeezed, each one contracts into a hexagonal, or honeycomb, pattern with its neighbours.

When the columns are curved it shows that the cooling surfaces were not parallel to each other and the columns were obliged to bend in an effort to conform to the right-angle rule. The most spectacular examples are at the Clamshell Cave and Buchaille Rock in Staffa, and at Ardmeanach, in the walls and arches of caves near McCulloch's Tree.

Contraction sometimes squeezed certain constituents, such as Calcite, out of the basalt, into the fine vertical joints, as if the columns were cemented together.

On the south coast of Ulva the columns are most impressive, giving long stretches of shoreline an artificial appearance, like the walls and foundations of ruined buildings. In fact, one site in Ulva is known as 'the Castles'.

THE STRUCTURE AND CLIMATE OF MULL

MCCULLOCH'S TREE

Dr McCulloch was the first to describe, in 1819, the 'fossil tree of Burgh', regarded by the geologists of the Scottish Geological Survey in their memoir on Mull (1924) as 'the most arresting single geological phenomenon in the island'. It is one of the natural wonders of Europe. It is the cast of an ancient coniferous tree trunk, 40ft (12m) high, embedded in the lowest lava flow of the cliffs at Rudha nan Uamha (Point of the Caves), a hundred yards north of the double waterfall of Allt Airidh nan Chaisteal, the most westerly point of Ardmeanach.

When the first flow of lava spread across the ancient land surface which was covered with forests, McCulloch's Tree was engulfed. Yet it exerted just enough cooling influence and resistance with its bulk (it is nearly 5ft (1.5m) in diameter) to preserve its outline in the solidifying flow. The lowest 3ft (90cm) of the trunk survived, fossilised by siliceous water, and the original grain of the wood can be traced on the surface. In a cavity at the side a quantity of the original charcoal is still to be seen, apparently as fresh as when the tree was charred by the great heat millions of years ago.

The local cooling influence of the tree modified the vertical jointing pattern of the surrounding columnar basalt, which is curved from the vertical to the horizontal within the last 3ft (90cm) of the trunk. Over the ages the cliff has been cut back until the cross-section of the tree now stands exposed. On looking down on to the horizontal 'cart wheel' formations on the flat worn rocks of the shore, the observer can speculate that he or she is looking at the eroded horizontal (instead of vertical) cross-sections of other ancient trees, with the columns radiating out from the cooling centre like the spokes of a wheel.

Those who face the long difficult walk to the tree are warned to arrive there at half-tide or on a falling tide, or risk being cut off for hours at the base of the cliffs. They are also invited by the National Trust for Scotland, which owns this area, known as The Wilderness, to call at Burg farm on the way and report their intention to visit the tree and obtain exact directions.

THE STRUCTURE AND CLIMATE OF MULL

THE QUINISH TREE

In 1984 a peculiar pipe, or column of rock, was discovered on the rocky shore below high-water mark near Quinish Point, in the extreme north of Mull, by Tommy Maclean, member of an old Dervaig family. He described it to the writer of this book, who examined and photographed it and sent details, with rock specimens, to the Hunterian Museum (Department of Geology) in Glasgow and to the British Geological Society in Edinburgh. While expert examination of the find is still to be carried out, the opinion is that this is indeed an important discovery and that a fossil tree has been discovered in a new area in Mull. Similar formations have been found in Tenerife.

It is the cast of the trunk of a tree, 24ft (7.3m) in length by 20in (50cm) in diameter, cut through at one point by a fracture or geological dyke which has displaced 3ft (90cm) of the trunk. Further exploration in the area revealed several smaller stumps protruding from beds of ash or tuff; and 12ft (3.6m) from the original tree there is the long outline of another tree deeply embedded. All the trees are lying flat along a line north-east to south-west unlike McCulloch's Tree (see page 00), which was massive enough to remain upright in the flow.

The Quinish trees are considered to have grown on the weathered surface of an early lava flow between periods of volcanic activity, and been overwhelmed by the next flow. It is possible that this horizon extended over the whole Mull area and that the Ardtun leaf beds (see page 21), McCulloch's Tree and the Quinish trees were contemporary and simultaneously covered by a widespread extrusion of lava and ash. Sealed into the flow and preserved by their sappy content, the casts of the Quinish trees remained as open 'pipes' after their woody content had disintegrated with the passage of time. These pipes, like crevices and spaces in the lava flows, were infilled under extreme pressure by a later flow, or from nearby geological dykes, whose material was of a harder chemical nature than that of earlier flows. Hence, when massive erosion removed the overlying lavas, the more resistant casts of the trees emerged as we see them today.

The Quinish area is much more accessible than the site of McCulloch's Tree, being no more than a pleasant walk of 3 miles from the village of Dervaig.

ECONOMIC GEOLOGY *Granite*

The Ross of Mull granite of the Assapol/Fionnphort area is a decorative and useful rock, pink or red in colour, which can take a high polish. It was quarried commercially for forty years up to the beginning of the twentieth century, when, because of competition from mainland granites the industry declined. Thousands of tons of Mull granite were shipped around the world, particularly to North America.

The Mull granite could be split readily into large blocks, and were ideal for massive building works such as docks, bridges and harbour walls. The main quarry, now abandoned, is at Tormore, half a mile north of Fionnphort slipway.

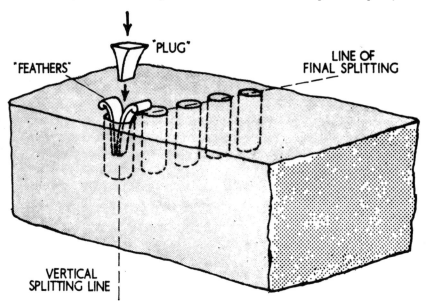

In the 'plug and feathers' method of splitting granite a series of iron wedges (feathers) were driven with the aid of iron plugs into a row of holes bored in the rock until it split under the pressure along the line of holes

25

It stands a few hundred yards inland from a lovely beach of white sand. Here are the ruins of the pier from which the blocks were shipped. They were conveyed there from the quarry by a steep tramway. Large stockpiles of blocks are still to be seen, some of the blocks as much as 10ft (3m) long by 3ft (90cm) square. All the work of cutting and finishing was done by hand.

The original method of splitting the granite was the time-consuming one of driving dry wooden wedges into cracks and holes and expanding the wood by constant soaking with water. This was superseded by the 'plug and feathers' method introduced from the Mourne quarries of Northern Ireland where it was first adopted in about 1860. For this a line of holes 1½in (38mm) in diameter and 6in (15cm) apart was drilled in the granite. Two thin iron wedges, the 'feathers', were inserted in each hole, forming smooth walls between which the plug, an iron wedge, could be driven. The plugs in the row were then hammered down in turn until the rock was forced to split along the line of the holes.

One giant monolith, called locally the Prince's Monument, is still lying in its bed in the face of the rock opposite the main quarry. This was to have been erected in London in the last century as an obelisk in honour of the Prince Consort. However, a flaw was discovered and the project was abandoned in favour of a different style of memorial, which stands in Hyde Park, and which is partly built of this granite. Many of the public buildings and works of our large towns were built of Mull granite, for example, Blackfriars Bridge, Holborn Viaduct and the Albert Memorial in London; Liverpool Docks; Jamaica Bridge in Glasgow; and Ardnamurchan, Skerryvore and Dhuheartach lighthouses off Mull. It also provided the fine polished facings of many imposing buildings. Curling stones, most attractive in appearance, were also made and for a time were in great demand, until superseded by the use of closer-grained granites from Ailsa Craig in the Firth of Clyde and from Wales latterly.

Sandstone
There is a bed of hard grey sandstone exposed on the shore

below high-water mark below the Nuns' Cave at Carsaig. This was an excellent medium for cutting and shaping into ornamental stonework, such as is seen in the original carvings in Iona Cathedral, in the facings of old chapels throughout the island, and in recumbent tombstones. This quarry was first worked by the monks of Iona. The stone at Carsaig was last worked in 1873 and was used later in the restoration of the abbey in Iona.

In this case, as the stone was covered at high tide, the use of wooden wedges was simplified, although still slow. The slabs were carried up to the Nuns' Cave immediately above, where they were shaped before transportation. The floor of the cave has a thick layer of chippings below the detritus of the centuries.

There are other sandstones at Carsaig well suited for building work, and another outcrop at Bloody Bay, just north of Tobermory, but their commercial exploitation is inhibited by distance, labour and transport problems.

Silica Sand
At Gribun there is an outcrop of silica sand suitable for high-grade optical work; it is similar to the sand that has been worked extensively for such uses at Lochaline, in Morvern, on the mainland, since World War II. Unlike the Morvern one, the Gribun outcrop is badly situated and has never been exploited.

Building Sand and Aggregate
There are a few useful deposits used in local construction work, such as the quarry near Torosay.

Road Metal
There is no shortage in Mull of sources of road metal, since the volcanic rocks provide suitable material that can be quarried almost everywhere, as can be seen from the many small wayside pits and quarries. Morainic gravels, pebbles, rotted basalts, and materials from hard and soft-textured dykes are widely used locally.

Coal

The thin seams of lignitic coal west of Carsaig have been thoroughly examined but their quality is poor and their accumulations irregular, and efforts to exploit the workings commercially would be highly uneconomic. In the past, tenants at Shiaba farm included coal in the payments for rent and for a time it was used at Pennyghael smithy, being conveyed there by horse and cart along rough moorland tracks.

The coal is much younger geologically than the carboniferous coals of the principal coalfields of the United Kingdom. However, its presence in Mull points to a long period of quiescence between two periods of volcanic activity, which allowed the coal-forming materials to be laid down in considerable thicknesses; for it takes about 20ft (6m) of peat measures to be converted into a 1ft (30cm) seam of coal by pressure from overlying rocks. There are further traces of coal at Ardtun, and Gowanbrae near Bunessan.

Peat

Geologically speaking, peat is a recent, post-glacial formation of organic materials that has been accumulating, layer after layer, under cool, wet conditions, in ill-drained bogs and marshy places. During the last few centuries its deposition has slowed down, probably through altered climatic conditions and improved drainage. It varies in texture from the black, compressed material at the foot of the deposits to the loose, fibrous upper layers. The black compacted type burns with considerable heat and a characteristic scent.

One remarkable property of peat is its preservative qualities. In the sterile peat measures, many organic items have been found preserved, such as 'bog butter', buried in the peat during the summer for use in the lean winter months but unretrieved because the markers were lost. (Bog butter is more common in Ireland.) Even bodies have been preserved for centuries, the most notable being the 'Tollund Man' discovered in deep peat in Denmark, the perfectly preserved body of a sacrificial victim interred in pre-Christian times.

THE STRUCTURE AND CLIMATE OF MULL

Semi-precious stones

On the hills and shores both north and south of Loch Scridain there are outcrops of sills containing crystals of corundum or sapphire. The sapphires are usually small, up to half an inch or so; but in a sill just beyond the Nuns' Cave at Carsaig, and immediately above the shore, they are found up to an inch or two across. However, they are thin, plate-like and impure, and are of no commercial value.

Iona pebbles and marble

Fine white marble exists in a 40ft (12m) wide stratum running north-north-west and south-south-east in the south-east of the island of Iona. It cuts freely, polishes well, and is durable, although it tends to yellow with age. It has been used for ornamental work through the ages: in early times an altar in Iona Cathedral was formed from a 6ft by 4ft (1.8m by 1.2m) block of marble, and was referred to by Sacheverell, Governor of the Isle of Man, in 1688. It disappeared piecemeal as a result of the superstition that a fragment of the altar carried in a boat averted shipwreck.

Early in the nineteenth century the marble was quarried extensively, but demand tapered off and little work, if any, has been done since the beginning of the twentieth century.

On the south and west shores of Iona beautifully coloured pebbles are sometimes cast up by the action of the waves. The most famous type is known as the Iona pebble. Seldom exceeding an inch or two in length, it is found on the shore at Port na Churaich, especially after stormy weather. It is an attractive green variety of serpentine, varying in colour from dark green to light greenish-yellow, and it is probably derived from serpentine nodules in an undersea extension of the Iona marble.

The softness of the texture allows Iona pebbles to be readily worked into curios and tiny ornaments which find a ready sale. Their attractive qualities have been known for centuries, for in 1688, during a visit to the island, John Fraser, Dean of the Isles, compiled a quaintly comprehensive description which he presented to Sacheverell:

Here the sea casteth up in ane place a number of small stones of divers collours and transparents, verij fair to look upon. They realy are peculiar to the place, for the longer they lay on the shoar they reapen, and turn more lively in their coulors. They yield to the file and admits of good polishing and engraving. Marble also of divers collours and with beautyfull vains is found on the island. It has been counted renouned, pairtly for the gouid discipline of Columbus [sic] who is buried in it, and pairtly for the monuments of the place.

CLIMATE

Mull shares the climate of the western seaboard of Scotland, with cool summers and mild winters. Snow rarely falls, and when it does come it soon disappears except on the northern slopes of the high hills. The incidence of frost, too, is negligible in comparison with mainland conditions. These circumstances reflect a combination of factors. The prevailing winds are westerly or south-westerly and the air brought to the island has been warmed by its passage over the comparatively warm waters of the North Atlantic Drift that flows out of the Gulf Stream; hence the amelioration of winter conditions. The configuration of the island allows the penetration of moist, warm air. In summer, as the earth warms up, the surrounding waters exert a cooling influence on the land temperatures and Mull thus benefits by its very insularity.

Despite its northerly situation – about 56′30″N – the arrival of spring, as signified by the first flowering of certain plants, comes as early in Mull as it does, say, in the Cheshire Plain or Humberside. Similarly, Mull enjoys a very long growing season for vegetation, some seven to eight months, during which the temperatures do not fall below a critical level.

However, exposed as it is to the Atlantic gales, the island receives both a large amount of rain and strong winds, and the narrow glens tend to funnel the wind into the central areas. In Glen More, for instance, in addition to the customary stout stays used to anchor them, the telegraph poles were set, in certain places, into foundations of logs sunk deeply into the soft bogland; otherwise they would have been flattened to the ground or torn right out.

Mull is wetter than any of the other Hebridean islands.

METEOROLOGICAL DATA FOR TIREE

Temperatures in °C (°F)

	Jan	Feb	Mar	April	May	June	July	Aug	Sept	Oct	Nov	Dec
Monthly mean	5·3 (41·5)	5·2 (41·4)	6·3 (43·3)	7·8 (46·0)	10·1 (50·2)	12·2 (54·0)	13·7 (56·7)	13·8 (56·8)	12·6 (54·7)	10·4 (50·7)	7·9 (46·2)	6·4 (43·5)
Monthly mean maximum	7·0 (44·6)	7·2 (45·0)	8·5 (47·3)	10·3 (50·5)	12·9 (55·2)	14·9 (58·8)	16·1 (61·0)	16·3 (61·3)	14·9 (58·8)	12·3 (54·1)	9·7 (49·5)	8·1 (46·6)
Monthly mean minimum	3·5 (38·3)	3·2 (37·8)	4·0 (39·2)	5·2 (41·4)	7·2 (45·0)	9·6 (49·3)	11·2 (52·2)	11·4 (52·5)	10·3 (50·5)	8·4 (47·1)	6·1 (43·0)	4·7 (40·5)
Absolute maximum	12·2 (54)	11·7 (53)	15·0 (59)	17·8 (64)	22·2 (72)	25·6 (78)	26·1 (79)	24·4 (76)	21·1 (70)	18·3 (65)	14·4 (58)	13·9 (57)
Absolute minimum	−6·7 (20)	−6·7 (20)	−6·1 (21)	−4·4 (24)	−0·6 (31)	2·2 (36)	6·1 (43)	5·0 (41)	1·7 (35)	0·6 (33)	−3·9 (25)	−5·0 (23)
Sea temperature	7·8 (46)	7·2 (45)	6·7 (44)	7·2 (45)	8·9 (48)	10·6 (51)	12·8 (55)	13·3 (56)	13·3 (56)	11·7 (53)	10·6 (51)	8·9 (48)
Sunshine index[1]	16	26	32	40	47	39	30	34	33	26	21	14

[1]Percentage hours of sunshine/hours of daylight.

Records of rainfall have been kept for a long period at three points in Mull and at one in Iona. These records show that average rainfall per year varies from 81.3in (206.5cm) at Auchnacraig (near Grass Point, in the extreme east), which is in the lee of the mountain core of the island, to 48.4in (122.9cm) in Iona. Although the latter is in the most exposed westerly position, because it is so low-lying the moist air does not give up its rain until it is cooled by rising against the central mountains. On Ben More and other high places the annual rainfall reaches 125in (317.5cm), an amount equalled in the Hebrides only by a small central area in the higher and more massive Cuillins of Skye.

From the average of the four sets of rainfall records over a period of thirty-five years, May is shown to be the driest month, with only 3.66in (9.3cm). Thereafter the monthly average rises to a maximum of 8.4in (21.3cm) in October. This is merely an arithmetical average for the whole island, however; rain must be expected right through the year, with the smallest amounts in late spring and early summer. Moreover, most of the stations are situated at only limited heights above sea-level. Gruline, at the foot of Ben More, with an annual average of 79.8in (202.7cm) more closely reflects the heavy precipitation of the adjacent mountain mass. There are local variations in the incidence of rainfall, depending on the height above sea-level, the character of the soil and even of the vegetation, notably the extending woodlands. Peat-covered areas are commonly waterlogged, and produce locally humid conditions; sandy areas are quickly drained and drier; the transpiration from lush vegetation in damp areas returns more moisture to the atmosphere and renews the cycle of rainfall, drainage and the taking-up of water by plants.

The moderating influence of the surrounding waters and of the warm North Atlantic Drift is perhaps best illustrated by the relatively small range of temperatures that Mull experiences. The annual range of temperature – that is, the difference between the means of the warmest and coldest months – is about 9°C (16°F). This contrasts with annual ranges in the Grampians, at about the same latitude, of over 11°C (20°F) and in the Home Counties around London of over

Page 33: Loch Frisa from Achnadrish Hill on the Dervaig road

Page 34: Sea-worn columnar basalt on the Ardtun shore of Loch Scridain, looking across to the trap country of Ardmeanach

14°C (25°F). Sea-surface temperatures in these waters average 8°C (46°F) in winter and over 12°C (54°F) in summer; maximum and minimum temperatures are reached later in the sea than on the land.

No official records of temperatures on Mull itself are available. Conditions are fairly similar, especially in the west central area, to those on the island of Tiree, 24 miles to the west, where meteorological observations have been recorded since 1931. According to Tiree's records, July and August are the warmest months, with the latter slightly the warmer. The highest absolute temperature recorded in Tiree was in July – 26.1°C (79°F). January and February are the coldest months with temperatures down to about 5°C (41°F) – comparatively mild in relation to East Coast temperatures, around the Firth of Tay, of less than 3°C (around 37°F). Average temperatures in the hills are, of course, lower than those of the lowlands.

The duration of sunshine is naturally related to cloudiness and therefore to rainfall. Mid-July, a notoriously wet time, may be expected to be rather cloudy. This generalisation is confirmed by reference to the meteorological data for Tiree; a sunshine index can be calculated by expressing the monthly mean of hours of recorded sunshine as a percentage of the possible hours of sunshine (ie hours of daylight). The July index is 30 per cent; that for May is 47 per cent, for June 39 per cent, for August 34 per cent and for September 33 per cent. Certainly May and June and late August to September are periods to be recommended for visits to the island. However, on the whole, Mull probably enjoys as much sunshine as the south-west of Scotland.

Up to early June the irritating attentions of midges, clegs and the common house-fly are absent, and the bracken has not yet reached its full development – in places it can reach over 5ft (1.5m) in height, which means that it both conceals objects of interest and makes the going hard off the beaten track. In August and September the heather is in full bloom and the early autumn colourings are superb. For the angler, salmon and sea-trout should be established in the lochs and rivers they frequent and brown trout are back on the take after their mid-season off-period.

2 FLORA, ENVIRONMENT AND WILDLIFE

BETWEEN 1965 and 1970 the Department of Botany of the British Museum conducted a survey of the flora and environment of Mull, in which 5,280 species and varieties in over 1,600 genera, including those mentioned in all known records, covering the 450 square miles and a similar area of the surrounding seabed, were specified. Obviously space permits no more than a brief review of the survey and interested readers are strongly recommended to read its detailed findings: *The Isle of Mull: A Survey of its Flora and Environment* by the Department of Botany, British Museum (Natural History), edited by A. C. Jermy and J. A. Crabbe.

Mull was chosen as a survey site for a number of reasons. Its flora has both island characteristics and affinities with the flora of the mainland, occupying a pivotal point on the west coast of Britain between the southern oceanic and the northern mountain flora. A wide range of habitat was described, as well as of land use. This is the most intensive botanical review of Mull ever undertaken. Subjects include: flowering plants and conifers; ferns and their allies; liverworts and mosses; lichens and fungi; freshwater algae and diatoms; marine algae and diatoms.

HABITAT

Habitat is delicately balanced and depends on a whole series of factors: geology, especially the chemical composition of the rocks; differences between the soils of the plateau lavas, the central volcanic complex, and the granite and schist of the Ross of Mull; depth and drainage of the soil; exposure to wind and salt spray; temperature, elevation, rainfall, incidence of frost and snow; running water; influence of the tides on shallows and saltings; and the presence of man, domestic animals, birds and wildlife.

For instance, the high percentage of nitrates round the nesting places of sea-birds encourages abundant growth of the common sorrel (*Rumex acetosa*) and chickweed. Pignut (*Conopodium majus*) and wood sedge (*Carex sylvatica*) grow freely on old woodland sites, while former swamplands encourage the growth of reeds (*Phragmites australis*). Again, a rare species found only in Mull and in the Isle of Skye is Iceland purslane (*Koenigia islandica*), which seems to owe its existence to a delicate balance between rapid freezing and thawing in salt-laden winds at a certain elevation. Another plant, rare in Scotland, which is found in Mull, is fool's parsley (*Aethusa cynapium*). At the other extreme, lack of basic nutriments in otherwise favourable conditions can lead to a restricted habitat.

The presence of man has a marked effect on plant life. Plants escape from cultivation and thrive in the wild, such as herbs in part of the Ross of Mull that were grown in the Middle Ages by the famous Beaton doctors. Hemlock is another example, and flax is a survivor from the days when it was actively cultivated. In Iona – a rewarding island for botanists – deadly nightshade (*Atropa belladonna*) was a drug-plant used by the monks in the Middle Ages. Old mortared walls, with their high lime content, have their special plants. The ruined walls of the nunnery in Iona carry a remarkable show of blossoms in season. Embankments along the new roads have a new rich growth of white clover. Sheep, cattle and goats influence soil fertility and habitat, and the un-restricted growth on the Treshnish Islands shows the wide difference between grazed and ungrazed lands. Even the building of a reservoir, or using a loch as a water supply, can have its effect: note the disappearance of pipewort (*Eriocaulon aquaticum*) when Loch Staoineig, in Iona, was brought into use as a water supply. Nettles spring up wherever man has lived, even in ancient forgotten sites among the hills, through the presence of trace elements and nitrogen from ashes, refuse, etc left in the soil.

The result of the extensive area of land in Mull above the 1,000ft (305m) level is the presence of arctic alpines (32 per cent). The Isle of Skye, with ten times as much land above this height, has 45 per cent.

Weather plays its part. Rain distribution is more important than the total precipitation. On open sites the number of wet days per annum varies from 200 to 220 on average, a wet day being defined as precipitation of 0.04in (1mm). Fogs and sea mists prevent evaporation and encourage lush plant growth, while the tendency of clouds to form on the leeward side of the hills after late summer affects the distribution of certain species of alpine plants. Another notable result of high local rainfall is the leaching of soil, with a long-term effect on plant growth and species.

There is a great variety of mosses and fungi. In particular, sphagnum moss, in a number of species, forms a deep and springy carpet over the boglands. In damp pastures and marshy places many species of the orchid family are found: frog, fragrant, butterfly, pyramidal, purple, spotted and marsh orchids, (names related to appearance, colour, or characteristics), and there are several species found only in Mull. Mosses and fungi are particularly abundant in the clean, pollution-free atmosphere on the eastern side, where humidity is greatest and the winds are more free from their salt content.

Marine plants follow much the same pattern of habitat as the terrestrial: shelter from or exposure to ocean currents, geology of the sea floor, upper and lower tide limits, sand, light, salinity (which is less as the coast is approached), and oxygen content, which increases where streams flow in – all have their effect. As far as the chemical analysis of freshwater lochs is concerned, this conforms to Scotland as a whole.

Bracken

Special mention must be made of bracken (*Pteridium aquilinum*), the menace to the stock-raiser. It grows most freely on brown forest soils 10in (25cm) or deeper. In sheltered hollows it can grow into a veritable jungle 5ft (1.5m) in height. Its upper limit of growth, at 1,000ft (305m), marks potential forest limits, both past and present. On well-drained soil it spreads quickly and soon smothers grasslands. Certain modern chemical sprays are effective eliminators, but highly expensive to apply. In former times, with the greater availability of manpower, the growing shoots were scythed in early summer for at least three consecutive years, which discouraged growth.

The spread of bracken in the last 150 years can be attributed to a change of land use. Prior to this period, the grazing of the many cattle, and of the smaller number of horses, trampled down and held the bracken in check on hill pastures. If grazing is scanty cattle will also actually eat young tender bracken shoots. Then the cattle were replaced by sheep, which avoid the bracken, which soon swallows up their pastures. Again, bracken fronds were stored for bedding down cattle and horses in winter, thus augmenting the supply of manure for spring cultivation, as well as for protecting potatoes stored in the open, which were first covered over with dried bracken and finally covered with a layer of earth to allow winter rains to run off.

Types of Soil

From the time when Mull assumed its present form after massive erosion, soil with the chemical constituents of the underlying rocks began to gather. Glaciation swept away the weathered surface, depositing the detritus in places protected from the main ice stream. Subsequently the local rocks slowly began to break down, depositing a layer of soil over the whole area. A study of the rocks today reveals the following analysis.

Plateau basalts (covering 45 per cent of Mull) give a brown, loamy soil, very suitable for cultivation, grazings and woodlands. Mull owes its green hilltops to this type of soil, which turns to peat over hard rocks. The central mountain complex (35 per cent of Mull) consists of alluvial gravels and sandy loams, allowing some cultivation, rough grazings and forestry on terminal moraines and alluvial deposits. Ross of Mull granite (5 per cent) yields an undulating, ridged, rocky landscape, with shallow soil and clay pockets, loam and deep peat, suitable for rough grazings and some cultivation. Schist

(3 per cent) produces clay loams with extensive cultivation, rough grazings and forestry. The rock surface is more friable. Raised beaches (4 per cent) give a gravelly, sandy soil, allowing extensive cultivation and rough grazings.

Organic soils contain over 20 per cent of organic matter and exceed 10in (25cm) in depth. Where they become water-logged, oxygen is excluded, decomposition is restricted, and most of such soils qualify as peat.

Moors and Grasslands

Long exposure to grazing by cattle, sheep and deer has led to considerable change in moorland vegetation. In general, the purple moor grass (*Molinia caerulea*) gives its typical colouring to the grasslands at an altitude of 500–1,000ft (150–305m), notably on the trap landscapes of the west and south. It is the dominant species, tussocky in nature, smothering other plants. It grows well over peat, avoiding stagnant areas, and its quality is improved by burning off the dead grass in the spring. On the higher moorlands (over 1,000ft/305m) and in the more acid soils of the central area the vegetation is typically that associated with the fescue and bent (*Festuca agrostis*) of the sheep-grazing moors. It is poor grassland, growing better on the sandy valley moraines of the central complex.

Moorlands and steeper slopes carry a widespread growth of ling heather (*Calluna vulgaris*), and bell heather (*Erica cinerea*) is abundant. In the damper areas the cross-leaved heath (*Erica tetralix*), with its delicious fragrance, is plentiful, along with bog-myrtle. White-flowered ling ('white heather') in little clumps or single sprigs can be found by the observant searcher in young, well-established growths on the drier hill-slopes.

The common ling has deteriorated during the course of the twentieth century. The reasons are partly climatic and partly related to disease, but the decline can particularly be attributed to the lack of rotational burning, which should take place every fifteen to twenty years to create a healthy regeneration, and to careless burning. Skilled management of heather moors is necessary if they are to be used profitably as sheep or grouse lands, which depend on young, healthy growth.

Summary
Scrambling along the rocky shore at low tide can be as rewarding as searching the hills for white heather, for there are so many things to be observed. The different species of seaweed, for instance, include two forms of red algae found at low tides – dulse (*Rhodymenia*) and carragheen (*Chondrus crispus*) – both of which are edible, with a rich, salty tang. There are the creatures of the rocky pools, the beauty of empty shells, the flotsam of sea life and items carried by the sea from far places. There is the artistry of the waves carved into the rocks.

Inland, the blossoms are richest in late spring and early summer. At first the undergrowth in the damp woodlands is carpeted with masses of wood anemones and wood sorrel, with primroses, wild violets and wild hyacinths, followed by a riot of wild flowers. Clumps of toadstools grow among the deep mosses and on the rotting wood of old birch trees, and the fresh green shoots of the larch trees contrast with the darker spruce. Summer has the fragrance of the fragile dog-rose and wild honeysuckle; everywhere in the boglands there is the unforgettable scent of bog-myrtle and bog-mint. Autumn brings the purple of the heather, blending with the rich colourings of the dying bracken fronds. Wild fruits are plentiful, especially brambles (blackberries), raspberries and strawberries, the last often growing to the size of a large hazelnut with an acid sweetness more delicious than that of the cultivated strawberry. In October hazelnuts are plentiful, especially in south-facing sheltered hazel thickets.

WILDLIFE

The largest native mammal in Mull is the red deer, estimated at about three thousand head. They are found high up on most of the hills and concentrated in the sporting estates at Torosay, the Ben More 'forest', and the Laggan peninsula. They can be a nuisance to farmers when they descend to lower levels to nibble growing crops, while within plantations they damage and destroy young trees by biting out the tender tops and ring-barking. Commercial deer farming is a possibility, but it depends on such factors as sufficient acreage to carry a viable herd, extra supervisory staff, and capital investment in handling, storing and exporting carcases. There is a herd of fallow deer in the woodlands around Knock and Gruline, while roe-deer are also present in Mull.

Brown and blue hares (the latter growing a white coat for winter) are present in Mull. They were unaffected by the disease, myxomatosis, which almost wiped out the hordes of Mull rabbits in the early 1950s, as they do not live in burrows (as rabbits do), where the disease was most virulent. Dean Munro wrote in 1569 that rabbits were present in great numbers in Mull and Inch Kenneth. Tradition has it that they were first observed on the sandy machair above the beach at Calgary, where the sight of the strange beasts aroused apprehension and curiosity among the people. As elsewhere in the country they became a major liability to farming, fouling the ground around their extensive warrens and ruining the grazings for livestock. On one hill farm the stock of young cattle was increased by 50 per cent after myxomatosis took its toll of the rabbits.

Of course, rabbits were a useful, if monotonous, addition to the islanders' diet, and were exported profitably to the mainland. There is the story of a visiting minister, who after a meal of stewed rabbit called on the man of the house to give thanks after eating. The words of the grace feelingly summed up the crofter's attitude to rabbits:

> Rabbits young and rabbits old;
> Rabbits hot and rabbits cold;
> Rabbits tender and rabbits tough,
> I thank the Lord I've had enough.

Unfortunately, rabbits are once again beginning to spread widely over the island.

Up to 1800 there were no moles in Mull. According to the *Statistical Account* of 1845, the first pair was accidentally brought into the parish of Kilninian in a load of earth ballast from Morvern. Moles have now spread all over the island.

Stoats and weasels are common, and polecats – sometimes confused with ferrets that have escaped and bred in the wild – have reappeared since the 1950s. Wild goats are still to be found on some of the high coastal cliffs of Ardmeanach and the south coast of the Ross of Mull. They are the descendants of domestic goats kept by former generations which either escaped or were turned loose at the time of the Clearances.

Field mice, wood mice, voles, shrews and rats are all common in Mull. Otters are common round the shores, and in some of the lochs and waterways, but their number is at a steady level and presents no problem. True, they do take a toll of trout and salmon but their favourite food is eels. All the coasts of Mull, especially along the Sound of Mull, are frequented by the common seal, while the Treshnish Islands have a breeding colony of grey seals that gather on the flat rocky platforms just above sea-level for mating and breeding from August onwards. Unlike the otter, the seal can be a menace to the stake nets of salmon fishers along the coasts. In such a precarious economy, the destruction of hundreds of pounds worth of nets, and escaped or mangled salmon – all the work of a single seal – can impose considerable financial hardship on salmon fishers. The number of seals must not be allowed to increase.

In the warm damp summers there is a vast amount of insect life, especially around the marshy margins of lochs, ranging from the dragonfly to the midge. The latter is a very real pest to both man and beast from mid-June onwards during windless weather. While midges can be found anywhere except on the cool hilltops or out on the water, their favourite haunt is along the line of drying seaweeds at upper tide limits. It is recommended to use a proprietary protective cream and a light headscarf during humid windless conditions. House-flies are another pest, although painless. The bites of horse-flies or clegs will often drive deer from one grazing area far up into the high tops while cattle take to cool waters, if convenient, or plunge deep into birch or hazel thickets. Many species of moths, butterflies, beetles and other insects are widespread.

Mull has its share of reptiles and amphibians: frogs, toads, newts, tiny lizards, slow worms and adders. The adder is the only species of snake found on the island. Although adders are quite common, they are rarely seen, for they are timid and vanish at the vibration of a footfall. If approached quietly they may be seen basking on sun-warmed rocks, old walls, heather, even on the tops of bracken and on large tussocks of purple moor grass. It is advisable to carry a stick and not to tread too softly when following paths through heather or bracken, for adders can become torpid and lazy when with young in hot sunny weather in late summer. The largest adders seen by the author never exceeded 32in (81cm), but as a rule they are about 24in (61cm) in length. The effective striking distance of an average adult adder from its coiled position has been proved by experiment not to exceed 10–12in (25–30cm). They like to frequent the margins of lochs and marshy places where frogs, their favourite food, are most abundant. The bite of an adder has little effect on a healthy adult beyond some slight discomfort for a day or so.

BIRD LIFE

The great variety of bird life in and around the island attracts enthusiastic ornithologists to Mull. Bird-watching is a hobby, and a pair of good binoculars brings a new dimension into the study of wildlife. According to an authoritative count, 203 different species of birds have been seen in Mull, from the wren to the golden eagle. Some are rarely seen, many are resident all the year round, but most of them are seen during particular seasons; for instance, at breeding times, when they are wintering on the island, or when they are simply passing through to other destinations. Rather than take up space with lists that might well be incomplete, it is suggested that anyone interested should contact the British Trust for Ornithology, or the Scottish Ornithological Club (21 Regent Terrace, Edinburgh) for full information.

Most interesting of the birds is the golden eagle, which is now becoming fairly numerous, nesting in some of the more inaccessible corners of the island. Its great wing-spread and magnificent soaring habits are a source of admiration. The sea-eagle (or white-tailed eagle) has been reintroduced to the island of Rhum, where several pairs are brought over from Scandinavia each year and have become firmly established. It is larger than the golden eagle, and is sometimes seen over Mull. The sea-eagle was harried to extinction in the Western Isles before the middle 1800s, and the golden eagle just missed the same fate, for these birds had gained the exaggerated reputation of being predators on livestock, especially on young lambs. Buzzards are common and can at first be mistaken for golden eagles until comparison shows up their smaller size and lower flight. Other birds of prey include the sparrow hawk, kestrel, merlin, peregrine and hen harrier. We must not forget that cunning member of the crow family, the hooded ('hoodie') crow, which is hated by farmers and shot on sight (if it can be approached) for its habits of attacking helpless sheep and lambs weakened or bogged down at lambing time.

Cuckoos find Mull an ideal place to visit. As many as seven or eight have been counted within a few hundred yards in early summer, each with its attendant meadow pipit.

Perhaps one of the most fascinating sights is a sample of the bird life on the Treshnish Islands (a natural bird sanctuary) in late spring and early summer. Here there are established colonies of many varieties of gull, and of puffin, guillemot, shag, cormorant (locally called 'scart', from the Gaelic *sgarbh*) and other species. The cliffs echo with their noisy clamour; the ground is littered with rough, untidy nests, while the narrow ledges of the sheer cliffs host the burrows of puffins; grass, rocks and cliffs are whitened with bird droppings. Wild geese halt here to browse on the rich grass covering the islands.

Mergansers and the great northern divers take their toll of trout in the hill lochs, and an angler need hardly set up his tackle if one of these wary birds has been there before him.

Along the rocky shores the piping of oyster-catchers – St Brigid's bird – and redshanks echoes back from the cliffs. Shags and cormorants stand tall on the off-shore skerries with outstretched wings, enjoying the warm sunshine, their crops replete with fish.

Grouse used to be fairly plentiful in Mull; now their coveys are rarely seen. The bird lives on the flowers of heather, but much of the heather has become coarse, woody and out of

45

3 THE PEOPLING OF THE ISLANDS

THE prehistoric people of Mull were part of the successive waves of early migrants from the southern and central European mainland, mostly by way of the Atlantic sea route between Ireland and south-west England. Piecing together the story can be done for the island, through the interpretation of archaeological finds, but a comprehensive and systematic survey of Mull has never been carried out. The Royal Commission on the Ancient and Historical Monuments of Scotland undertook a survey of the ancient monuments, and its findings were published in 1980: *Argyll: an Inventory of the Monuments, Volume 3 – Mull, Tiree, Coll and Northern Argyll*. The island of Iona is excluded.

In trying to reconstruct Mull's prehistory one must remember that, as elsewhere in the Western Isles, the island was probably occupied intermittently at times, after the retreat of the ice, and that, when settlement became more continuous, new arrivals, whether coming peaceably as colonisers or traders, or coming as pirates or in war, commonly became intermixed with the aboriginal and then indigenous folk. Thus one finds a slow change in cultures, as new technologies were brought in, and a gradual intermixing of racial types and of their habits, customs, religious beliefs and language. Such assimilation would be of a greater or lesser degree, depending on the degree of dominance of the incoming people, but it was likely to continue even after the later Celtic and the Norse invasions.

THE EARLIEST SETTLERS

The first human to set foot on Mull may have belonged to a family of late Stone Age hunter-fisher folk who crudely worked

47

tools of bone, antler and stone, and whose kitchen middens of limpet shells have been unearthed in two cave shelters near Oban, at a former beach level when the sea stood 25ft (7.6m) higher than it now does. They lived by strand-looping – sailing from one bay to the next.

The first settlers on the island, therefore, were likely to have been Neolithic colonists, arriving during the third millenium BC – perhaps they found a few aboriginal savages still inhabiting that part of Scotland's western seaboard. Neolithic settlement can be assumed to have continued on Mull, quite possibly with some temporary breaks, for as much as a thousand years, and gradually to have given way to a more advanced way of life as the use of metals became widespread. The island may have seen a fair amount of traffic during those two thousand years or so up to the centuries before Christ, though little evidence has been unearthed to prove it in detail. But between the years 2500BC and 600BC the island must have had some attraction for the Bronze Age peoples. Its basalt soils were richer and less acid than those of the Outer Isles, even though workable sites may have been limited to a few lowlands; moreover, it stood near the south-western approach to the Great Glen, a natural trade route.

The way of life of Mull's small settlements during this period would be based on a combination of cattle raising and crops, varied by fishing, shellfish collecting, and hunting wild animals such as deer, horses or wild ox.

There are in Mull several relics of this culture in the form of megalithic sites of various kinds. Over the broad span of time, roughly between 2500BC and 600BC, there spread over western Britain and into the islands a cult that involved the building of stone monuments, circles and cairns, of which the landmarks of Avebury in Wiltshire and Callanish in Lewis are well known. The origins of this, like those of Mull's crop cultivation, probably lay in the Middle East, arising from the Egyptian cult of the dead, for the cult spread, via the Mediterranean and south-west Europe, through Brittany to the north-west. The megalithic monuments and the attendant rituals that the missionaries introduced to the Bronze Age settlements were doubtless acceptable since they would meet both the religious needs of these early folk and their need for a seasonal organisation of their economy, thus giving the priesthood control over the native peoples.

Several sites in Mull have been examined and recorded by Professor A. Thom, who lists their localities and form in his *Megalithic Sites in Britain*. His list includes the following: Quinish (alignment); Dervaig (three sites – two alignments and a group of three stones); Glengorm (standing stones); Tobermory (alignment); Ardnacross (alignment and two stones); Duart (menhir and stone circle); Ross of Mull (menhir); Dail na Carraigh (cairn, alignment and two stones); Ardalanish (two stones); Uisken (cairn or tumulus and menhir); Loch Buie (stone circle, possibly a cairn or tumulus). There are, of course, many lesser examples throughout the island.

They are mostly composed of standing stones and stone circles, some sited in remote parts of the moors, others near contemporary settlement sites in the lowlands. Most of the stones are deeply embedded in the turf; others are quite hidden under accumulations of peat; many have been removed as convenient building material and in dry-stone dykes. One such stone, part of an incomplete stone circle, can be seen built into the east wall of the new cemetery at Kilmore, above Dervaig, a convenient substitute for one ton of building stones! Of the two well-preserved stone circles at Loch Buie, one is 44ft (13.5m) in diameter, the other just under 22ft (6.7m).

In his analysis of the British megalithic sites Thom shows that there is a wide variety in the actual shapes of the 'circles'. The arrangements of the standing stones and stone circles are shown to be in accordance with observations and sightings of various heavenly bodies – sun, moon and certain first-magnitude stars – such that they provided a calendar, accurate and permanent, for fixing the date of the solstices, the passage of 'months' and even of hours. They also incorporated a unit of measurement, the megalithic 'yard' that, it is suggested, has a relationship with the Spanish unit of linear measurement of that and later periods. Conclusions as to the purpose and use of the monuments may reasonably be assumed to be connected with rituals concerning worship, death and the farming calendar, such as seed-sowing, animal slaughter and fertility.

Below Craig a'Chaisteal, a mile west of Calgary Bay, there is a flat area of ground below the road known as the Druids' Field. It extends to the edge of the cliff and must once have been divided by a stout wall, the sunken remains of which can still be traced. In the field are two boulders, whose flat, west-facing sides are covered with cup-shaped hollows about 2in (5cm) in diameter.

The megalithic sites may be seen as a reminder of Mull's participation in a widespread culture that encompassed almost the whole of Ireland and the western coasts and islands of England, Wales and Scotland well over 1000BC, and also of the high level of intellectual achievement of the missionary-priests who attached themselves to the existing settlements and came to dominate them. No similar interrelated system of landmarks was laid on the country until the Ordnance Survey imposed its network of triangulation across the landscape in the nineteenth and twentieth centuries AD.

The individual settlements of Mull were self-supporting, scattered communities, tied to the lowlands and evolving under the influence of newcomers and traders, and exploiting to the full the local environment. Many of the archaeological finds related to them were probably connected with burials (cremation was then the practice). Among these finds are gold ornaments found at Torloisk, including a penannular ring and a dress fastener with ornamental ribbing, and a sun disc in copper, 3in (7.5cm) in diameter, with lines of engraved dots and circles. Thin, knife-like blades of bronze were found at Callachally in Glen Forsa among sepulchral deposits. Pottery sherds have also come from lower Glen Forsa. The lowlands around Salen have produced several finds, including a flat adze of the early Bronze Age. A cist found there was associated with flint blades, bronze fragments and parts of a string-marked pottery beaker. Another cist at Quinish contained an urn or food vessel 5½in (14cm) high, with string-marked ornamentation, and at Sunipol, near Calgary, a similar urn held a skull and a stone axe. Stone axes and flint arrowheads have also been found in this vicinity. Some archaeological finds may be seen in Mull houses and a few inns, and also in the Tobermory museum opened in the early 1970s.

Another kind of archaeological evidence, the remains of crannogs (lake dwellings), probably dating also from the period known as the late Bronze Age, serve to remind the observer that peasant refugees were known in Britain – and in Mull – in the centuries before Christ. Crannogs were a highly developed form of settlement, with a high standard of living, found around the Swiss lakes about 1000BC. A worsening of the climate and rise in water levels forced these peoples, with their domestic animals, families and belongings, to become involved in the tremendous movements of people across Europe that were then developing, with the spread of Iron Age cultures and the increase of warrior tribalism, some to seek refuge, along with other migrants, in Britain. It has to be guessed whether some families eventually reached the Western Isles, or whether the *idea* of living in a crannog, a defensive form of settlement with a natural moat, was passed on by other migrants coming to the north-west. It is also possible, of course, that the idea of a crannog was evolved locally.

There are at least six known lake habitations: in Loch Ba, Assapol, Poit-i, Frisa, Sguabain and Loch na Mial (2 miles south of Tobermory). Some are of the stone-cairn type – an accumulation of stones sunk in the loch until they reached the surface and on which an artificial island was built. Others were built on a framework of logs lashed to piles driven into the floor of the loch, with an infilling of brushwood and stones. They were usually connected with the shore by a zig-zag causeway of stepping stones just covered by the water, designed to mislead and discourage intruders. Some of the islands are quite large, up to 85ft (216m) long. When Loch na Mial was partly drained in 1870, not only was the original crannog exposed, the existence of which had previously been unsuspected, but the causeway leading to it was found, under 4ft (1.2m) of silt. Two dug-out canoes, one of which was 17ft (5m) in length with a beam of 3ft 6in (10.5m) were also discovered.

THE PEOPLING OF THE ISLANDS

THE COMING OF THE CELTS

The building of crannogs may have heralded the next, more violent, stage in the history of Mull's people. Already incursions of Iron Age peoples from central and southern Europe were reaching southern and eastern Britain, pushing before them people they had ousted from their settlements. This was a time of intense pressure on living space, when populations expanded rapidly and iron implements made the task of clearing new land and fashioning more effective weapons easier. It is also the period when the Celts, as peoples, enter the local scene. At this point let us comment on the pronunciation of the word 'Celt'. It has become fashionable to pronounce it 'kelt'. Ignoring the fact that a kelt is a spent salmon, the hardening of what is a soft lovely word is deprecated by such authorities on English pronunciation as H. W. Fowler.

T. G. E. Powell, in a chapter on the coming of the Celts in Stuart Piggott's *The Prehistoric Peoples of Scotland*, reminds us that they were a transalpine people known to the Greek and Latin classical writers as early as the late sixth century BC, one of the barbarian peoples admired by the Romans and identifiable by their characteristic appearance, arms, manners and customs. They were iron-using farmers and stock-raisers; they were widespread across Europe, powerful and warlike. With growing populations everywhere creating land hunger, and with the political and military upheaval that accompanied the growth of the Roman Empire, Celts became involved in the outwards migrations and reached Britain as invaders, bringing a new Iron Age culture. They reached Scotland both by land from the south and by sea on the east and west, and Mull may then have received its first hostile invasions. While it is known that the Celts fused with the indigenous Bronze Age settlers whom they overran, much as earlier migrants had done, they were a dominant element, stamping their language and way of life on the territory they took. The megalithic monuments probably continued to be used for their ritual purposes, for, at the dawn of recorded history, as Caesar reported, a Celtic druid priesthood existed.

52

Their religion was by now probably a compound of ancient Bronze Age beliefs and other practices added in more recent times, and it may have provided something of a unifying force among both invaders and invaded.

The first colonies of Irish Scots were probably planted in Mull during the early part of the second century AD; by the fifth century the island was part of the Scots kingdom of Dalriada, embracing Argyll. About this time, during this Celtic assertion from Ireland towards the east and north, Britain had moved from prehistory to history and the Celts themselves were adopting Christianity.

During the Iron Age the later waves of more militant invaders from Ireland were strongly opposed by the earlier and more settled incomers, who erected many defensive works in strategic positions round the coasts – chiefly on the western and southern sides. They were in use as late as Viking times against the sea-rovers. What may have been prehistoric permanent settlements, visible today as ruins almost level with the turf – for example, Reudle, a little inland from the north-west coast of Loch Tuath, and Suie, near Bunessan – are attributed to the period.

There are more than three dozen duns or forts which served as defensive watch-towers beside settlements, or as strong-points where attackers could be delayed while the people and their livestock withdrew inland. Most of the duns and forts are close to the sea, though a small fall in sea-level, or uplift in the land surface, since that period may have changed some locations so that they now appear inland. Many stand in sight of each other and warning signals by fire could easily be transmitted. Some, like Dunara at Glengorm, were occupied up to medieval times. Dunara, in fact, was a substantial building that succeeded the dun, often described as Mull's fourth castle.

The ruin of a typical fort stands at Dun Aisgean, about a mile west of Burg, Torloisk. About 35ft (10.7m) in diameter and circular in shape, its walls were 6–8ft (1.8–2.4m) thick, with narrow horizontal openings at regular intervals. It stands on a boss of rock rising from the 100ft (30.5m) raised beach above Loch Tuath, with a convenient inlet below for a haven.

It had good arable land around it, now given over to bracken and sheep. If one looks down from the walls early in the year, before the bracken growth has started, one can see the outlines of a dozen or so old houses. Their age can only be conjectured, for this was a settled corner of Mull up to the middle of the eighteenth century.

A simpler type of construction on a crag at An Caisteal, between Bunessan and Loch Assapol, has been described in some detail in the *Proceedings* of the Society of Antiquarians in Scotland for 1927. The flat top, 200ft (61m) above sea-level, is 35ft (10.7m) across and strongly protected by dry-stone walling on the exposed flank, a typical Iron Age fortification. The wall is up to 13ft (4m) thick, with traces of a gallery and cell within its width, and an entrance 5ft 6in (2m) wide. It is so much overlooked from near-by positions within range of bow and sling that the threat it was designed to resist must rather have been sword and spear at close range. It was probably not a form of residence but a look-out post and fighting platform without the upper defensive walls or breastworks possessed by other duns. Much of the stonework has been plundered for local building, and this area, including the ruins, is now under accumulated peat up to 14in (35.5cm) deep. Excavations have revealed two small sherds and fragments made from very coarse clay, an upper rotary quernstone of mica schist, very much worn, nearly 14in (35.5cm) in diameter, and a triangular piece of mica schist some 6in (15cm) across with a cup-shaped depression, thought to be the upper bearing stone of a drill.

Dun Muirgheidh is a different type of fort about 2 miles from Bunessan and less than half a mile from the main road to Kinloch. It stands on a promontory on the south side of Loch Scridain. On the landward side it was defended by three walls built from cliff to cliff, with a central passage. The inner defensive wall was 17ft (5m) thick, with a check and bar-hole at the entrance. There is evidence in it of a passage and a mural cell. The final defence was a light wall. Dun Ban, or Glacindaline, a tidal island off Ulva, was a natural defensive point supplemented by a dry-stone wall, with a boat inlet and a causeway designed like the approach to an ancient crannog.

Among the different styles of duns and forts there was the Gallic fort, in which the dry masonry was bound with timber lacings, and it has been suggested that the vitrified forts that have been found are Gallic forts with their stone walls fused through the intense heat of the timber when burnt either by accident or design. One example may be Dun Urgabul, lying beside the road to Glengorm less than a mile from Tobermory.

Brochs are specialised structures, rare outside the territories of the broch-folk of the northern Highlands and Islands. They were towering structures presenting a smooth outer surface of closely fitting stones, rather like a squat modern cooling tower. Ten thousand tons of stone could be used in the building of a large broch. They were double walled, with stairs and chambers within the thickness of the walls and an open court in the centre. They were probably the residences of leading family groups where neighbours, along with some of their livestock, could take refuge for short periods, for the forts were virtually impregnable when the entrance was closed up. Two brochs have been identified in Mull. One is An Sean Chaisteal, at Ardnacross, below the Tobermory–Salen main road. It is the usual circular shape, with walls 13–14ft (4–4.3m) thick and a central courtyard 34ft (10.4m) in diameter. There was a light defensive outwork. The other, Dun nan Gall (Fort of the Stranger), stands at the edge of the rocky shore on the north side of Loch Tuath at the south-east end of Ballygown Bay. Its internal diameter is 35ft (10.7m) and the walls are 11–13ft (3.3–4m) in thickness. There are traces of a gallery outside the fort. The 4ft (1.2m) entrance is on the east side, expanding inside to a door check and bar-hole. There are still remnants of a staircase 3ft (90cm) wide within the walls, and a guard chamber. Both structures are very much broken down.

The Treshnish islands, Cairnburg Mor and Cairnburg Beag, have fortifications dating from medieval and later days built over much earlier structures. In Glen More there are two cairns, Carn Cul Ri Erin and Carn Cul Ri Alabyn – respectively the cairns with their backs to Ireland and Scotland. (Alabyn – Albion – the land of the Picts, from *alb* or *alp*, a high hill, and *inn* or *innis*, an island. The name, originally

4 *CLANS AND CASTLES*

The historical records of Mull may be said to start with Columba's coming to Iona in about AD563, a story that warrants treatment in a separate volume (even though Iona is part of the Mull group). But the existence of the monastery in Iona in some measure affected Mull's own history because of the attraction that its manuscripts, relics, precious ornaments and caskets, and more practically its stores of food, had for the Norse pirates who began to harass the Western Isles at about this time. These raids escalated in intensity, not only on Iona (the community there was ravaged six times between 793 and 986), but on the small farming settlements, especially on the west coasts. That was when the many Iron Age forts were still in use.

It was about AD800 that certain factors in Norway led to a movement of people westwards. The population was expanding, leading to a land shortage exaggerated by the system of land division which operated against younger sons. There appears, too, to have been a climatic deterioration, with a succession of poor summers and bad harvests, and some unusual migration of fish from Norwegian waters to the west. Added to that, the Norsemen were warlike and adapted to the sea rather than to the land. Finally, the independent Scottish tribes could not present a unified front to the sea-raiders.

MEDIEVAL MULL

In the Western Isles Norse colonisation continued to be dominant from the eighth to the thirteenth century and Mull shared this very formative period of cultural history. During this time the family-tribal organisation developed into the clan system, with patriarchal clan chiefs living like minor kings in their territories, united in a confederacy ruled by the Norse King of the Isles, a right won by the King of Norway from the Scottish Crown in 1098.

After the battle of Largs in 1263, the Norse kingship of the Isles ended, and Mull came under the administration of the Lordship of the Isles. The title Lord of the Isles survives to this day, the present holder being Charles, Prince of Wales. This Lordship of the Isles was a confederacy of seventeen clans under the leadership of MacDonald of Islay, who was or became through marriage both Lord of the Isles and Earl of Ross. This confederacy was a powerful and unruly faction, a constant thorn in the side of the Scottish Parliament, which was never forgiven by the MacDonalds for denying the strong claim to the Crown of Scotland of Donald Balloch. In 1476 the MacDonalds were forced to submit to James III, and the Celtic-Norse Lordship was abolished, although unrest simmered for some time afterwards.

Clan names originated in a number of ways. Some came from personal names such as MacDonald (son of Donald) or MacLeod (son of Leod), and so on. Others came from the trade or appointments of the progenitor, such as Macintyre (son of the carpenter) or Macnab (son of the abbot). (Lay abbots held church appointments.) Other clan names commemorate the characteristic of some progenitor, such as Campbell (twisted mouth) or Cameron (wry nose). Clans could be classified into four main groups roughly based on their geographical locations: Norman; Pictish; Norse; and Gallgael, or Celtic Scots from Ireland. Nearly all the leading Mull clans were of this Celtic extraction, as one would expect from the situation of the island – Campbell, MacDonald, MacDougall, MacGillivray, MacKinnon, Maclean and MacQuarrie. Since the eleventh century Norman lords (eg Fraser, Murray, Montgomerie, Sinclair) had advanced northwards into Scotland and been granted land by Scottish kings, displacing native chiefs.

Mull lay in a region in which many defensive castles were built during the medieval age of romance that saw the rise and fall of the Lords of the Isles. To this age of clan culture and ceremonial are attributed many of Mull's tales and legends.

Duart Castle

The name Duart means dark headland, and the castle stands in a commanding position on the first point of the island passed on the way from Oban through the Sound of Mull, the whole width of which could be swept by cannon fire in the old days. Originally, it was a MacDougall stronghold, build in the thirteenth century, and the old tower has walls of 10–14ft (3–4.3m) thick. It is now in two flats entered from the great central quadrangle, and has a hundred apartments. When the MacDougalls fell from favour because of their opposition to King Robert the Bruce, much of their land in Mull, along with Duart Castle, was forfeited and conferred on the Lords of the Isles. Later, the custody of Duart was transferred to Lachlan Maclean when he married Mary, daughter of John of Islay. When in turn the Lords of the Isles were punished by the Scottish Parliament, the Macleans of Duart were confirmed in the castle and former MacDonald lands in Mull, becoming one of the most powerful clans in the Western Isles and dominating the southern Hebrides. During the Civil War, however, the Macleans were in opposition to Cromwell and were duly punished. Duart Castle was occupied by Cromwell's forces, and the weakened Macleans were overrun by the clan Campbell on the doubtful excuse of non-payment of debts. From 1692 the castle was used as a barracks for government troops, gradually falling into disrepair and becoming ruinous. However, in 1911, Sir Fitzroy Donald Maclean, 10th Baronet of Duart and chief of the clan, with a distinguished army record, purchased Duart Castle with 400 acres (160ha) of adjoining land from Mr Murray Guthrie of Torosay. The castle was rebuilt, restored, and reoccupied as the home of the chief. It has been open to the public during the summer months since 1968. It is now the home of Lord Maclean, who was Chamberlain of the royal household and former Chief Scout.

Access to the castle is by a private road branching off the main road about 2 miles south of Craignure.

Aros Castle

Aros is a Scandinavian word meaning an estuary, as in Aarhus, Denmark. In this case the estuary is Salen Bay and the mouth of the Aros river. The ruins of this ancient and massive keep stand commandingly at the edge of a bold bluff just north of Salen Bay, 8–9 miles from Tobermory and near good arable ground. Aros is also the name of the postal district around Salen and also of the estate, which stretches as far as Tobermory. Reduced now to a few walls and masses of rubble, it was a substantial hall-house and bailey, with a defensive ditch and bank on the flat landward approach, where the ruins of a small chapel also remain. The great walls were massively rather than skilfully built to a thickness of 10ft (3m) or more. Like Duart, it was probably built by the MacDougalls, and conveyed to the MacDonalds, in whose hands it became the chief stronghold of the Lords of the Isles, together with Ardtornish Castle at Lochaline, on the opposite shores of the Sound. It followed the same sequence of ownership as Duart – after the MacDonalds, the Macleans and finally the Campbells of Argyll. An old tradition relates that the treasure of the Spanish galleon sunk in Tobermory Bay was recovered and still lies deep under the ruins of Aros Castle.

Moy Castle

Standing above the shoreline beside a small stream, at the head of Loch Buie, this castle was built, probably in the early fifteenth century by Hector Maclean, brother of Lachlan Maclean of Duart, and progenitor of the MacLaines of Lochbuie who made this their home. It has three storeys and a garret, and is more of a tower house than a strategic defensive centre like Duart and Aros. At floor level (which is solid rock) there is a well of good water which refills as fast as it is emptied, although with no overflow. A small pit prison, called a bottle dungeon, was built into the stonework, with access from the first floor.

Confiscated, like Duart and Aros, during the Civil War, and garrisoned by Campbell followers, the castle was later restored to the MacLaines but abandoned as a residence in

1752, when a new house was built, which Boswell described rather disparagingly during his visit in 1773. Although roofless, the castle is still impressive to view from the outside, but as a result of possible danger from crumbling masonry the entrance door is barred.

Dunara

Less accessible and not as impressive as the three principal castles, the ruins of Dunara stand on the flat summit of one of the small plateau lava outcrops near Sorne Point, Glengorm, with a convenient inlet for boat landings. The hall and numerous other buildings were easily defended by a curtain wall round the perimeter of the summit. It is considered to

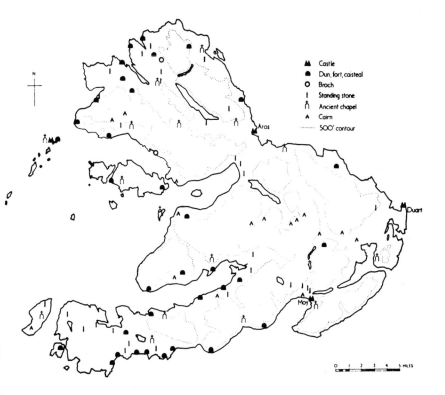

Sites of prehistoric and medieval remains in Mull

have been built by the MacKinnons, who held the lands of Mishnish as early as the mid-fourteenth century, but were later ousted by the Macleans.

Dun Ban
This is a small rocky tidal island between the islands of Ulva and Gometra, and is known as Glackindaline Castle. It is in an excellent defensive position with a good landing-place, and although built in the late medieval period it was a secure home for the MacQuarrie chiefs of Ulva until a more comfortable residence was built in more settled times. A portion of the walls of this later home is still standing at the estate office near the present Ulva House at the east end of the island. This old house is where Dr Johnson and Boswell were entertained by the MacQuarrie chief during their tour.

Cairnburg Mor and Cairnburg Beag
These are nearly impregnable fortress-islands. Cairnburg Mor and its smaller neighbour Cairnburg Beg, which was fortified to support its larger twin, are the northern outliers of the Treshnish Islands, off the west coast of Mull, which are described later. Cairnburg Mor was strategically situated to command the sea-lanes to the Inner Hebrides, although there is neither a safe anchorage nor a dependable landing-place on the strip of rocky shore on account of the stormy seas and tidal rivers running among the reefs.

Pennant's *Tour* of 1772 states that in 1249 John Dungadi was appointed by Acho, King of the Nordeneys (the northern sphere of Norse territorial claims in the Hebrides), to defend the two islands, and he held out for a long time under pressure, even after the Norse rulers had been expelled. Cairnburg Mor was known then as Kiarnaburgh, or Biarnaburgh. After the Treaty of Perth in 1266 it was regarded as a royal castle, and later the custody of it was transferred from the MacDougalls of Lorne to Angus Og (MacDonald) of Islay, and thereafter to his successor, the Lord of the Isles, a transfer which was confirmed by a Charter in 1343. In 1390 the custodianship passed to the Macleans of Duart, but in 1647 the island was captured by Commonwealth troops following the adherence by the Macleans to the Royalist cause. In 1608, again in the hands of the Macleans, it held out against the punitive fleet under Lord Ochiltree sent to subdue the rebellious clan chiefs. Maclean held the stronghold in 1715, although during the Jacobite uprising it was taken and retaken by both sides. It was finally surrendered to the Campbells of Argyll in 1692 when the power of the Clan Maclean weakened and Mull fell into the hands of the Campbells.

Formed as it is by the flat summit of a sea-girt plateau, dropping in 120ft (37m) cliffs into the sea on three sides and on to a narrow rocky beach on the north-east side, defences consisted of walling along the edge of the cliff rather than of massive buildings. Light cannon could fire from built-in emplacements through embrasures in the walling. Only one steep path was left to give access to the top through an entrance gateway, a death-trap for attackers, down which boulders could be rolled from a stockpile above. The defenders were accommodated in a narrow gully crossing the summit, which was roofed with timbers and turfed over. There is the ruin of a large, two-roomed, thick-walled house which was used as a refuge or a prison, as the case might be, in times of clan intrigues. Near-by is a small ruined chapel. Fresh water was obtained from seepage of rainwater dammed back to form a small pond which would have had to be protected from fouling by seabirds. On the shore there is a tiny rock basin called the Well of the Half Gallon which refills with good water exactly to its former level after it has been drawn upon – rather like the Moy well.

Cattle and sheep used to be grazed on the rich grass covering the plateau. Thick, tall nettles grow within the walls. Cairnburg Mor might be a rewarding place for archaeological research, for it is reputed that books, manuscripts and relics were hidden there by monks fleeing from Iona during the Reformation, although Cromwell's men and the Reformers are supposed to have searched the place and destroyed what they could find. Precious historical records may still be hidden there.

Cairnburg Beg follows the same pattern of defensive

measures, but on a lower and less ambitious scale, partly above the foreshore, partly on the upper eastern portion.

An old chapel, church or cemetery can be looked for wherever the prefix "kil-' appears. 'Kil' (in Gaelic *Cille*) originally meant the cell or habitation of the early missionaries and came to be applied also to the surrounding ground. Ancient chapels – all ruinous on Mull, unlike that of St Oran in Iona, which is restored – are scattered all over the island in seemingly haphazard fashion. When they were in use they were conveniently sited in relation to the many scattered communities of the time whose people thought nothing of walking many miles to worship. They were built mostly between the twelfth century and the Reformation and were constructed on a simple plan, of which Pennygown chapel (see below) is a typical example.

On Inch Kenneth are the remains of a church of the first pointed period, about 40ft (12m) by 20ft (6m) in area, with a piscina and, in the south-east, a ruined sacristy; the windows are deeply splayed lancets. Outside the north-east corner lies the grave of a medieval chief, Sir Alan Maclean, covered by the most elaborately carved slab in Mull. The effigy, in high relief, is in quilted armour, the right hand clasping a ball; a broadsword and dirk are worn; the left hand bears a plain shield and under the helmet the hair is long and curly. By the side of the head are the figures of a monk and a nun in attitudes of prayer. A hound lies at the feet. Old crosses and stones stand in the vicinity of the chapel.

The ruined chapel of Pennygown, surrounded by an old burial ground, stands beside the main road 3 miles east of Salen. The sides of the entrance have recesses for bars and hinges. Three narrow windows, with rounded heads, and the doorway are faced with sandstone from Gribun or Inch Kenneth. There is a recess about 3ft (90cm) square in the east wall. On the grassy floor of the building lie many plain flat tombstones of slate and schist, some covering a collection of human bones, doubtless dug up in the burial ground during interments. Close to the east wall stands the lower shaft of a broken cross of mica schist, of Celtic design, probably fourteenth century and brought from Iona. It is intricately carved with, on one side, the Virgin and Child and on the other a lymphad (galley) with furled sails surmounted by a design with foliage. Outside the east gable lie two very old grave slabs said to cover a chief of the Clan Maclean and his wife, who, according to tradition, were refused burial within the holy ground of the chapel itself because they had indulged in witchcraft and unholy rites. The original entry to the cemetery was by stone steps rising to the top of the boundary wall and descending on the other side, a device to exclude straying cattle.

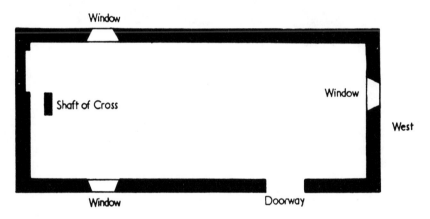

Plan of the remains of Pennygown Chapel, typical of medieval chapels in Mull. The chapel is 39ft 9in by 17ft

Tombstones

Carved recumbent tombstones dating back to between the thirteenth and sixteenth centuries, and sometimes even earlier, are to be seen in several of the older churchyards in Mull; they are a special attraction in Relig Oran, beside Iona cathedral, where they cover the bodies of early Scottish kings and dignitaries. The material used was often slate or schist slabs imported from the mainland, but in the Nuns' Cave at

Carsaig (used as a workshop by the monk stone-masons of Iona) many stones were shaped from hard sandstone slabs cut from the tidal quarry on the shore below. On the walls of the cave can be seen what appear to be trial carvings and holy symbols, and the trademark of an individual craftsman.

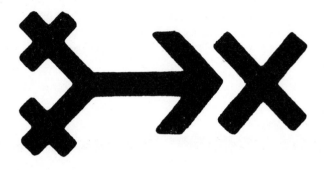

A symbol carved on the wall of Nuns' Cave, Carsaig, is considered by the Ancient Monuments Commission to be the trade mark of a mason or monk who worked there, possibly in early Christian times

Old tombstones were carved to a pattern which identified the person interred, or his pursuits. The cross and holy symbols are of course common to most, like the skull and crossbones to signify mortality. Sword and galley indicate a maritime clan chief; the sails of the galley are often furled to show that a voyage has been ended. If the legs are crossed, the man has been in the Crusades to the Holy Land. A huntsman was represented by a dog in pursuit of a hare, and symbols of fishing or falconry were similarly used. A woman is identified by shears, mirror, comb or harp on her tombstone, while the clergy are marked by chalice and bell.

Other very old tombstones can be seen at Tobermory, Kilninian, Kilmore and other places in the south of Mull; too often they are neglected, and obscured by moss or grass. In south-eastern Mull, the nearest point to the mainland, there were several landing-places, and faint traces of sections of old tracks can still be found. They seem to start and end without

Page 67: (above) At the foot of the 1,000ft Gribun cliffs runs this road threatened by landslips: (right) The 700ft high cliffs west of Carsaig Bay, with sandstones overlain by thick basalt flows

Page 68: (above) Curving basalt columns on the shore below a 150ft cliff on the western headland of Ardmeanach; near this point lies the track down to the shore level which leads to McCulloch's Tree *(left)* about half a mile north. This 40ft high cast of a tree is fossilised in a lava flow

connection, but they were old paths converging on the pilgrims' route. Names like Port nam Marbh (Port of the Dead) point to alternative landing-places to which the bodies of the dead were conveyed by a number of different routes across Scotland, and finally carried by galley across the Firth of Lorne.

THE CLAN SYSTEM

A clan can be defined as 'a social group or an aggregate of distinct families actually descended from a common ancestor, and received by the King, through the Lord Lyon King of Arms, as an honourable community'. The clan system has been called 'the finest example of benevolent feudalism in Europe'.

The original family tribal system that evolved into the clan system was at its most effective in the fifteenth and sixteenth centuries, but from then onwards it began to break up under increasing pressure from the Scottish Parliament. After the Jacobite uprising and following the Union of the Parliaments, the British Government systematically destroyed what remained of the clan system. Note that clan chiefs owed their allegiance not to Parliament, but direct to the king, which led to much of the unrest among the Highland clans when the royal line of kings deviated from what was held to be the correct and traditional line of succession.

Within the social hierarchy of a clan the chief held the clan territories in trust for his clansmen. While he himself might not necessarily be a man of means, his people were proud to maintain his standing in a manner worthy of the head of their clan. He was adviser, judge, protector, and military leader in times of armed conflict, whether national or caused by disputes with other clans (or sometimes even over a real or imagined insult, for they were an exceedingly proud race). To the chief the clansmen owed in return customary duties, including the obligation of military service. This obligation and kinship ties were features of the Gaelic society that survived the breakdown of the system itself, as witnessed by the response in later centuries to army recruiting calls in the islands under the chiefs – now turned lairds or landlords – and by the continued sense of clanship and recognition of chiefs today.

A chief could be described as a benevolent autocrat. In him was vested the right of summary jurisdiction, where as judge and jury he could condemn a malefactor to 'pit and gallows'. Another entitlement mentioned by Dr Johnson was the case of the MacQuarrie chief of Ulva. Even in the eighteenth century MacQuarrie retained the right of *merchata mulierum*, whereby a clansman had to pay his chief, if required, a fee of 5s on the marriage of the clansman's daughter. This was in substitution for the very old Norman practice of *droit de seigneur*, under which the chief or baron was entitled to spend the first night with the bride.

The chief of one of the larger clans lived and travelled like a little king. He had his 'seannachie' (the 'wise man' and story-teller), his harper, piper and attendants who included even a man called 'Wet Foot' whose role was to carry his chief across the streams dry-shod; and of course there was the armed bodyguard. In fact, the traditional hospitality extended to the party when travelling was a sore drain on many a family.

The clansman would readily lay down his life for his chief and obey his lightest wish, not in servility as might the serfs and villeins of feudal society, but as members of a family obeying a patriarch. Boswell related a story in illustration of this. A clansman in Iona was suspected by Sir Alan Maclean, his chief, of having evaded an order to provide some rum, and was pointedly reminded of his chief's powers of summary justice. Hurt by this lack of trust the man confided in Boswell, 'Had he sent his dog for the rum I would have given it. I would cut my bones for him.'

There was much that was good in the system. There was no poverty; the chief saw to it that the old, the widows and the helpless were cared for. Destitution and despair arose only when the clans were broken up and dispersed, with no substitute for the father-figure who cared for the people. Of course, there were always the 'broken clans' made up of people rejected from or expelled by other clans, for criminals were not tolerated within a clan. Grimly enough, losses in manpower through the regular military and inter-clan feuding kept the population at a level which could be catered for by the pastoral economy.

The Macleans were of very ancient lineage, claiming descent from the kings of Ireland. Through intermarriage with the family of the Lord of the Isles, they were granted extensive lands in Mull, and ultimately their territory included the whole of the island, Morvern, Coll and other possessions. They were a noble clan – there was reputed to have been only one bad chief – Neil Munro summed it up thus: 'The MacDonalds were warriors, but it was the Macleans that were the gentlemanly fellows.'

The decline in fortunes of the Macleans began with their support of the Royalist cause during the Commonwealth, and was finally achieved through their strong Jacobite leanings. However, the Macleans were exempted from the government enactment of 1597 requiring all chiefs and landowners in the Highlands and Islands to produce their title deeds, as this was a subtle move to confirm the Macleans in their lands as a counterbalance to the influence of the still powerful MacDonalds. But by the end of the seventeenth century all the Maclean lands were in the hands of the Duke of Argyll, under whom, in the eighteenth and nineteenth centuries, improvements were introduced into Mull in an effort to establish industry, but with little success. By the mid-nineteenth century financial pressure obliged the dukes to part with most of the Mull lands. Similarly the MacQuarries, who had held the island of Ulva for eight hundred years, were obliged to part with their lands for economic reasons by the end of the eighteenth century.

The way of life within the clan system in Mull was based on a cattle economy, and the breeding and export of beef cattle was the only source of real hard cash – apart from the boom in kelp which will be discussed later. Drovers undertook the herding of the black cattle across the island by traditional drove roads still traceable on the OS maps of Mull. But the sixteenth century saw the beginning of the disintegration of the clan structure of the Gaelic society of Scotland, and power and control over clan life were gradually removed from the chiefs by the Crown and the government, most forcibly after the 1745 uprising.

With the natural growth in population came pressure on the available land resources and by the mid eighteenth century a marginally balanced economy became a precarious one. The introduction of potato growing had eased the food shortage but contributed to the rising rate of population growth. There was no accompanying provision of new employment or expansion of the arable area. Indeed, in many townships the old communal system of runrig crofting gave way to independent holdings on the arable land, which became more and more fragmented with division among the family.

The islanders were not practised in any industry other than their pastoral farming and its ancillary occupations like cattle droving and fishing, and in the material terms of the national economy of the time they were extremely poor as well as overcrowded. In spite of the terms of the Treaty of Union of 1707, nothing was done to restore the scarce and debased Scottish coinage, and the islanders found barter a convenient means of exchange. Stevenson worked the poignant facts of the shortage of money into fiction in *Kidnapped*, in which David Balfour, making his way through the Ross of Mull after being shipwrecked, had to resort to the house of a 'wealthy man' in order to obtain change for a guinea piece to pay for a night's lodging.

Five and a half miles along the Glenaros road from Dervaig there was an open-air market, near the watershed and about two hundred yards left of the road, at an important focus of drove roads. This was Druim-tighe-mhic-ghillie-chattan (the ridge of the descendants of the Cattanach fellow), perhaps the longest place name in Mull. In rough huts of turf and around low turf tables, whose outlines can still be traced on the moorland, domestic goods were exchanged or bartered for, at what amounted to a regular country fair, where little money entered into the transactions. Not far from the site is a huge isolated boulder called (in Gaelic) the Bargain Stone, where transactions were discussed and settled. Unfortunately, this old market site is now trenched and planted behind the fence of the Forestry Commission.

Commerce began to develop towards the end of the century as landowners demanded a higher return for their land than the crofting rents produced. This led in turn to the incautious and wasteful exploitation of both the land and its people, even though some lairds were thoughtful about the welfare of their tenants. Human need and human greed are inextricably mixed in the unhappy events of the later eighteenth century and in the nineteenth century. Famine and pestilence there had been many times before, but in early times the people were resilient – they had land and their community life helped them to recover. Those days were now long gone and there followed the historical processes that are reflected in the island's present-day difficulties.

Mull's population rose to over eight thousand by 1801, and was steadily rising, with probably well over a twofold increase in a century, and that in spite of the large numbers of early emigrants who left the country in the 1770s to join the flow of people from the Highlands and Islands to North America, and of others who were recruited into the army.

5   *MODERN HISTORY*

The story of the Clearances is well known. Briefly, the sequence of events was as follows: clan chiefs replaced by new generation of landlords, often absentee, who through need or greed demanded hard cash for rents instead of part-time services and goods; attractive offers of high cash rents made by Southern flockmasters for introduction of sheep; eviction of tenants with no legal rights of tenure; clearance of houses to make way for sheep; destitution, migration and emigration for the people; collapse of the sheep economy, followed by creation of sporting estates; permanent depopulation, loss of good land and end of an old way of life. In Mull the only representatives today of the old clan chiefs are the Chief of the Clan Maclean, the Duke of Argyll, and descendants of the Macleans of Torloisk and Pennycross. By 1810 Lowland sheep flocks had become established over extensive areas of the Mull grazings, displacing the crofters' cattle and sheep stocks. The kelp burning for a time absorbed some of the surplus labour and around the coasts produced a bare living for some of the islanders, though at a dreadful cost in living and working conditions.

The island population continued to increase, reaching 10,612 by the time of the 1821 census, a number that included soldiers returning from the Napoleonic wars. The names of 116 officers alone are recorded as having come from Mull to fight in those wars. There must have been many hundreds of men in the ranks, now returned to find the old way of life largely gone, their homes threatened by eviction and their future livelihood in jeopardy. By 1825 the kelp-burning industry had collapsed. For the rest of the century, as the living standards of the islanders fell, the size of the population dropped steadily.

As a boy, the writer was told by an old man that he remembered well being carried, as a child, on his father's back out of the family cottage in Ulva, which had been built by the hands of his forefathers. The factor and his men were standing outside the door with blazing torches in their hands which they thrust into the thatch as soon as the people were out. This was a common story wherever land was taken for sheep. It was the age of Victorian privilege and hypocrisy on the part of people in high places.

One of the stoutest advocates for the setting-up of a government commission was Alexander Mackenzie, editor of the *Celtic Magazine*. He raised the question with a Member of Parliament in 1877, who brought the matter forcibly before the House of Commons. The Crofters' Commission of 1883 was forced by increasing public pressure to delve deeply into the cruel wrongs done to the people; in fact, in a period of six months it had to consider no less than 46,750 questions. Mull was considered by the Royal Commission (Highlands and Islands) of 1892, which was convened 'to find out what the desire of the people was in the way of land and to ascertain what land there is available for crofts and other small holdings'. The *Proceedings* make sad reading. Witnesses were examined, usually through an interpreter in the Gaelic tongue. In Mull alone the testimony of one man of undoubted respectability presents a shocking indictment. His evidence related to the north of Mull, but similar destruction of a way of life took place all over the island. According to his evidence, twenty crofters and three townships were cleared in Mishnish in 1842. Sorne (now called Glengorm) had a long record of earlier clearances which were completed by James Forsyth in the middle of the century with wholesale clearances of cottages and townships, and confiscation of grazings. In Calgary four populous centres were cleared by the Marquis of Northampton in 1822. Treshnish had three fine townships cleared in 1862. The witness described how Ulva and Gometra saw perhaps the most wanton destruction of all. From what was the finest arable ground in or adjacent to Mull, producing and exporting some of the best potatoes in the Hebrides, 100 people were evicted by the owner, F. W.

Clark, between 1846 and 1851; they were soon followed by most of the inhabitants of these islands remaining out of a total population of 800.

The treatment of the tenants in Dervaig, on the Quinish estate, was both harsh and contemptible. Established in 1799 by the former laird, Maclean of Coll, at the head of Loch Cuin, Dervaig consisted of twenty-six houses built in pairs, each with its own ample garden and an outrun on the hill behind. In 1857 the new proprietor, James Forsyth, induced twenty-four of the crofters to sign a new lease; but he failed to explain that they were signing only for the tenancy of their houses and gardens, and no longer for the outrun, which reverted to him. This was a double gain for the unscrupulous laird, who was now receiving the former rents as well as use of the grazing lands. All that was left to support the people were the vegetable gardens.

In 1847 George Douglas Campbell became 8th Duke of Argyll. He was described as a cold, calculating, grasping man whose acts of oppression bear this out, certainly in the Parish of Kilfinichen. Thomas Johnston, in *Our Scots Noble Families*, sums up the matter as 'Robbery of the Poor Islanders'.

In 1847 the rents of Iona were raised in one step by 50 per cent; in 1860 common grazings were taken from the crofters; rents were doubled and ground was confiscated from some to provide grazings for a few vocal objectors. No compensation was paid to crofters for the houses they had built, for fields cleared and improved or for walls and fences erected. Holdings were from 3–4 (1.2–1.6ha) acres in extent. Forty-six families were reduced to living in poverty in one square mile, while at the same time five large farms were created from the confiscated lands. One crofter who lost most of his stock by the savaging of dogs belonging to the Duke's gamekeeper, who re-stocked and claimed compensation, was ejected from his holdings. Between 1841 and 1881 the population fell from 5,197 to 1,990, and poverty was widespread. Under close examination, James Wyllie, Chamberlain to the Duke, admitted that he knew little of the estate at the time he had revalued the lands by 69 per cent. All these actions contrasted badly with the efforts of the 5th Duke at the beginning of the century to introduce industry and effect improvements.

In Tobermory the land owned by and settled under the direction of the Society for Extending the Fisheries differed from the ordinary crofting lands; yet even here persistent efforts were made by the landlord to take over the grazings. Only by costly and repeated legal recourse were the tenants able to retain most of these lands. However, rents and feu-duties were forced up, to the hardship of the people. Here, as in other estates, objectors were victimised. At Tobermory two crofters who gave evidence – Donald Colquhoun and Angus McInnes – were deprived of their holdings.

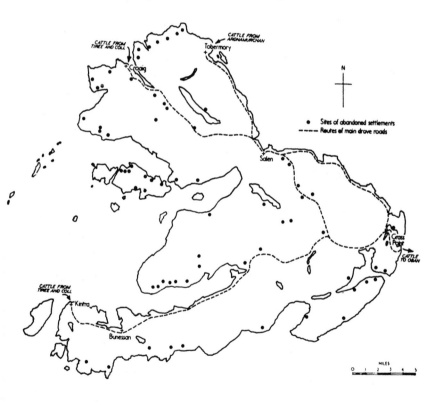

Locations of abandoned settlements in Mull. The routes of the main drove roads are shown; subsidiary tracks that connected settlements with these can still be traced and followed on the ground

In the lands of Lochbuie fifteen crofters were ejected from their lands and only two spared; hill grazings were confiscated. Here, between 1844 and 1894, the population fell from 546 to 252. The existence of indifferent absentee landlords was part of the cause.

It is not commonly known how Glengorm Castle received its name. James Forsyth, the laird of the Dervaig clearances, built himself a fine new house, one of the Victorian mansions erected in Mull at that time, and he sought to call it Dunara, after the ancient coastal fort in the estate. It was pointed out that this was not very appropriate, as the dun lay about a mile away. He then asked an old local woman on the estate for her advice. With bitter consciousness of the clearances that were going on, she replied: 'Call the place Glengorm.' The delight of the laird at this beautiful name would have been shortlived had he realised that its meaning – Blue Glen – would commemorate for all time the cruel days when the glen was indeed blue – with the smoke from burning townships.

In the early days of the Clearances Mull was certainly already overcrowded in relation to land resources and the pastoral economy. The Clearances in some form had to come; the tragedy lay in the manner in which they were carried out.

Destitute families converged on Tobermory and other villages. A meagre Poor Relief was accepted with shame; some found work making new roads. But poverty was widespread and many were in effect homeless. Famine added to their desperation after the failure of potato harvests in the mid-1840s, which caused a loss of what amounted to four-fifths of the food supply. In 1862 the poorhouse was built at Tobermory to accommodate the homeless.

In the fifty years up to 1871 the population of the island fell by a half and it continued to decline steeply until the turn of the century, many families emigrating to outposts of the Empire. In contrast to some of the outer Hebridean islands, Mull's peak of population was reached early in the century (1821), and rapidly declined possibly because the island is located closer to the Glasgow area with the opportunities there for employment and for transport overseas.

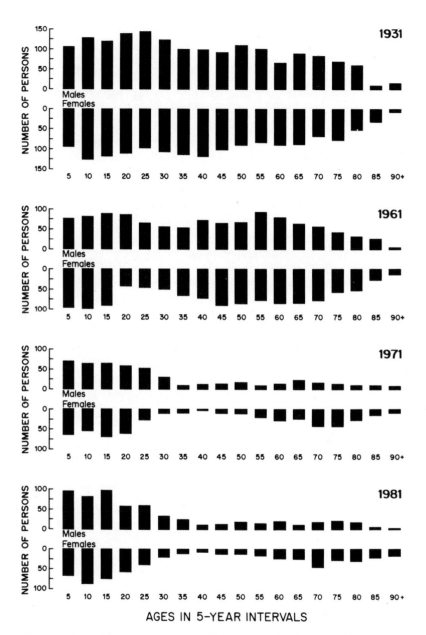

A comparison of the age structure of Mull's population in 1931, 1961, 1971 and 1981 illustrates the increasing imbalance. The number of persons in the younger age groups and those of effective working age have become disproportionately low, reflecting the emigration of people born in Mull in the inter-war years and the consequent low birth rate, as well as the need for those of working age to seek employment outside the island

MODERN HISTORY

DEER STALKING AND DISCONTENT

The Victorian fashion for hunting and shooting expanded widely, with improvements in sporting guns and rifles, as in communications. As a result, large areas now useless for grazing were turned over to grouse moors and deer stalking; in fact, grouse became the most sought-after game bird in the world. This activity developed in Mull in the latter part of the nineteenth century, contributing no real improvements in opportunities for the islanders, and bringing new landowners with even less knowledge of and interest in the social life of the islanders than their predecessors.

The sporadic rioting that occurred in some areas did not arise in Mull, though there was good reason for it to do so. The Crofters' Acts of 1886 and 1892 were intended to remove their grievances, chiefly by preventing arbitrary eviction and establishing security of tenure and protection against excessive rents for the small tenantry. But the legislation intended to improve crofting conditions did in fact create a rigid system and obstructed progress for the next hundred years. Grimble sums up the legislation thus: 'It has frustrated every attempt to solve the Highland problem during this century.'

THE TWENTIETH CENTURY

In Mull there was a temporary halt in the rate of depopulation around the turn of the century. But since 1911 the trend has been continuously downwards as the people have drifted away to mainland Britain and Commonwealth countries. The age and sex structure of the population has become unbalanced. Women outnumber men and the proportion of people in the older age groups is too great to support balanced economic progress. The deserted cottages and bracken-infested moorlands that we see today bear vivid witness to the fact that the island's inhabitants now number fewer than they did at the beginning of the eighteenth century.

The chief change in the landscape in the twentieth century has been wrought by the Forestry Commission, which started its work on Mull in 1924 and is now advancing its plantation boundaries rapidly on ground acquired through lapsed farm leases and the toll of taxation on overburdened estate owners.

In recent years the government, faced with the need to devise means whereby the Highlands and Islands can be helped to develop economic progress and restore life to decadent communities, has brought in legislation (The Crofters' Act of 1955) and established the Crofters' Commission (1955) and the Highlands and Islands Development Board (1965). The efforts of these agencies are slow to bear fruit. Mull is a microcosm of the whole region, and the survival of the island and of its remaining people depends on the achievement of such economic progress and social restoration.

6   *MULL AND THE SEA*

The traditional highway of the islanders of Mull was the sea, and Mull offered a safe harbourage, at Tobermory Bay, a fine natural harbour 30 miles nearer to the Hebrides and the open sea than Oban. Sea power and territorial power were closely bound together during the six or seven centuries between Columba's time and the subjugation of the Norsemen, and fighting ships and sea warriors must have terrorised the small communities on the island just as the Viking invaders terrorised the eastern shores of Britain. But commerce also played its part in the history of those and later times, and for Mull this also meant sea transport, both for trading locally and for more distant exchanges. The whole economy of the island is still, naturally, controlled by the availability of sea transport.

EARLY SHIPS

The earliest craft of which relics have been found are the dugout canoes discovered in Loch na Mial, near Tobermory. These were tree trunks, roughly hollowed or burnt out, and they are assumed to be of similar age to the lake dwellings where they were found. The Celts used coracles, unwieldy frameworks of wood and wattles covered with stretched skins, which were certainly being used at the time of St Columba (sixth century AD) and were much larger than popularly supposed. The coracle in which St Columba and his companions landed in Iona is believed to have been 60ft (18m) long.

The fine seaworthy craft of the Norsemen set a new pattern for boat-building in the Hebrides. A typical Viking galley of the tenth century displaced about 20 tons and measured 76ft

(23m) in length by 17ft (5m) beam. With high, carved prows and sterns, their draught was under 3ft (90cm) and amidships their free-board was no more than 3ft 6in (12.8m). They were clinker built (that is, each strake overlapped the one below, and the stakes were riveted together through small iron rivets), and their seams were caulked with cords of animal hair saturated with tar. Sixteen pairs of oars were carried, and the rudder was a large special oar blade on the starboard ('steer') side aft, and the mast, which carried a square lugsail, was amidships. The normal crew for a long voyage numbered about three dozen, but for local expeditions there were two or three men for each oar and an additional fighting crew.

A representation of the lymphad (gael. *long fhada*) or galley of the Hebridean and maritime clans was rendered in simple terms for heraldic purposes, on coats of arms (here of the Clan Maclean) or shields and tombstones of the island chiefs

MULL AND THE SEA

The Viking ship was the prototype of the craft used afterwards in the Hebrides, the galley, or lymphad, or longboat, and the smaller birlinn. The lymphad appears as a distinctly unseaworthy heraldic device on the shields and tombstones of the island chiefs, especially the clan chiefs of Mull. The Hebridean galley was fitted in time with a rudder instead of a steering oar, and was designed for two dozen oars. The birlinn carried up to sixteen oars.

When Mull came under the domination of the MacDonalds of Islay, these Lords of the Isles required a fleet of galleys to control their widespread possessions. About 1430, hundreds of galleys were involved in the rival fleets of Angus Og in a struggle against his uncle John, Lord of the Isles, and his allies. This was the most sanguinary naval battle ever fought in Hebridean waters, and the bay in which it was fought, just north of Tobermory, is said to have run red with blood – hence its name, Bloody Bay. Only a few years ago, in a tidal cave under the cliffs which encircle the Bay, skulls and human bones were found which may well have been the remains of some survivors of the fight, who took refuge there, only to drown at high tide.

TREASURE SHIP

In the next century foreign ships began to appear; none were more impressive than the storm-tossed survivors of the Spanish Armada which called in along the west coasts of Scotland and Ireland to refit. One of the most famous of these entered Tobermory Bay in September 1588, and its legendary treasure has been a source of speculation ever since. However, in 1986 Alison McLeay's *The Tobermory Treasure*, drawing on actual documents contemporary with the Armada made available for the first time from Spanish archives, presented the facts in their true perspective. This revealed that the galleon was not the *Florencia*, as popularly supposed, but a stout ship of 800 tons from Ragusa (Dubrovnick) the *San Juan Bautista*. Homeward bound with cargo she called in at Sicily, but was there arrested by the Spanish authorities, her cargo unloaded, and with a crew of 60 and 300 soldiers she joined

Page 88: (right) Grimly-carved slab in Kilninian churchyard, probably covering the grave of a Maclean chief of Torloisk. Showing kilt and broadsword and *clogaid*, or pointed helmet, it is typical of carving done by the monks of Iona at the Nuns' Cave, Carsaig

(left) The shaft of a cross standing in Pennygown chapel, carved with the Virgin and Child and an inscription (now illegible); on the reverse side is carved a very fine design of a galley with furled sail, vine leaves and tendrils (*Dr R.B. Maneely*)

Page 87: (*above*) Cup-marked boulder in Druids' Field below Craig-a' Chaisteal, near Calgary Bay; (*below*) Cairn surmounted by a cross at Pennyghael, with Ben More in the background and Loch Scridain. It commemorates the famous Beaton doctors, of fame throughout the Hebrides in the Middle Ages

Page 86: (*left*) Eas Fors, a waterfall on the north side of Loch Tuath, tumbling directly into a deep sea pool covered at high tide; (*below*) The remains of Dun Aisgean, an iron age fort near Burg, Torloisk, surrounded by dense bracken. In the right middle distance lie the narrow waters between Ulva and Mull and, on the skyline, the central mountains

Page 85: Two examples of volcanic activity on Mull: (*above*) at Calgary a vertical dyke cuts through lava flows and stands out on the cliff face between a raised beach and the present shore. The walls of the old pier shed were built onto the bottom of the dyke; (*below*) The Quinish Tree, discovered in 1984 and identified a year later by the author, is the cast of a recumbent tree infilled by a later flow of lava. The second such tree to be found on Mull, the first was discovered in 1819 by McCulloch, the geologist

the Spanish Armada fleet at Lisbon and was re-named the *San Juan de Sicilia*. She was under compulsory hire until she was destroyed by fire in November 1588 in Tobermory Bay.

Between 1683 and the 1980s about forty expeditions were sponsored. Apart from guns, ships' fittings, a few coins and pieces of plate – which may have belonged to the officers and crew – little of real value has ever been recovered. The operations conducted by the Duke of Argyll in 1643, employing the (for the times) highly experienced diver John Miller, yielded a sighting of dishes of silver and pewter, but failed to secure a golden crown secured by a chain. The diver also reported the presence of 'metal' on the seabed around the wreck. It may be that the 'treasure', if below the gun deck as supposed, was hurled far and wide by the explosion. The indefatigable Sacheverell noted in 1688 that during his visit salvage operations were going on, but he makes no reference to any spectacular finds. One handsome Cellini cannon recovered in 1741 stands outside Inveraray Castle.

Unfortunately, the desperate searches for treasure and the wanton use of explosives resulted in wholesale destruction of the hull, in places down to keel level. There is no published official evidence in the manifests or elsewhere that the treasure – said to have been the pay chests of the army of the Duke of Parma heading for a landing in England, and amounting to £30 million (Scots currency – £2/3 million sterling) – was actually on board. But successive Dukes of Argyll have never given up hope (ownership of the wreck and its contents vests in them) for when the 7th Earl of Argyll lived at the Court of Spain in 1588 he was sure something in the ship was worth a long search – and so the challenge remains.

EVOLUTION OF THE COASTER

The sea was the quickest and safest medium for transporting troops to police the Western Isles during troublesome times in the seventeenth and eighteenth centuries, for mainland roads in the west of Scotland were few and primitive. In 1609 (as recorded in the *Register of the Privy Council of Scotland*, Vol VIII, 1607–10) Lord Ochiltree was ordered to proceed from Ayr with a punitive fleet to subdue certain 'Rebellious and Insolent persons inhabiting the northern and western isles of the Kingdom committing certain barbarous villainies on each other without reference to God or Law'. Lord Ochiltree was also ordered to destroy enough of their shipping equipment, to restrict their future raidings and insurrections. The expedition achieved its objectives by enticing the principal chiefs in Mull and the surrounding district to come on board the flagship in Aros Bay, near Salen, and sailing away with them to the courts of the South, where they were placed on probation. They obtained their freedom by signing the Statutes of Iona (23 August 1609), measures by which the Scottish Crown intended to bring the Western Isles under greater control.

There was now freedom for commerce to develop. Larger and more seaworthy ships were required. Sloops, smacks, skiffs and fishing boats were built. Up the the middle of the nineteenth century Mull fishing boats were undecked, which made them more controllable on the exposed rocky coasts where the larger East Coast boats were unhandy in use. But in competition with the experienced fishermen from the new fishing communities on the eastern seaboard of Scotland, who were professional fishermen, unlike the Mull crofter-fishermen, the islanders found themselves outclassed, and fishing never became a major industry in Mull.

The smack, up to 45ft (13.7m) long, was the maid-of-all-work of the eighteenth century. Around Mull those boats carried passengers and assorted cargoes in all weathers. The skiff, much smaller and lighter, was used on sheltered inshore passages.

A pattern of regular transport routes began to emerge. Even in October 1773, when Dr Johnson and Boswell visited Tobermory, they found it a busy place, though only twelve or fourteen ships were at anchor there when often there were as many as seventy. Some of those vessels traded as far away as the Clyde, Newcastle and even foreign parts. By 1797 there were thirteen sloops based on Tobermory engaging in coastal trade around the coasts of Mull itself.

For centuries Mull people have been far-travelled. Before reliable transport became available, they were travelling regularly to Glasgow and the South in sailing smacks and skiffs, making long journeys in overcrowded boats across wide stretches of open sea. The lighter skiffs were rowed or sailed to Crinan, and from there – this was before the Crinan Canal was constructed – like the galley of King Haakon, they were manhandled across the isthmus to the sheltered waters of the Firth of Clyde. The larger boats faced the stormy passage round the Mull of Kintyre to their destination.

The traffic was seasonal. Many able-bodied people left the island to seek work on the rich harvest fields of the Scottish Lowlands for three months of the year. The return of those people, and of others returning on routine visits to their families, were times of great rejoicing.

In August 1822 Iona and the Ross of Mull suffered their greatest calamity of the nineteenth century. The smack *Mary*, of Iona, with a full complement of workers bound for the harvest fields, foundered after being run down off Greenock by the steamer *Hercules*. Only four people, a woman and three men, were saved, and the victims were buried in the old cemetery at Greenock. The loss of over forty breadwinners and people in the prime of life was a tragedy felt for generations in the Ross of Mull.

THE COMING OF STEAM

When steamboats appeared in 1821, their obvious advantages could not be denied. With the introduction in the twentieth century of the internal-combustion engine, the small hardy inshore craft became safer and more manageable.

The utilitarian 'puffer', or steam lighter, now obsolete, used to push its way into may a corner of Mull with assorted cargoes. It could manoeuvre through intricate channels between reefs into such tiny slipways as, for instance, Croig, near Dervaig; or to be beached high and dry on its flat keel at low tide on hard beaches where formerly carts, and latterly lorries, could come alongside and load up. A consignment of coal brought in the puffer for individual homes in a local community would be carted away and unloaded in separate piles for the people to collect at leisure.

91

MULL AND THE SEA

The inelegant puffer, with its blunt bows, was little more than a floating hold, with its engine right aft and a mast forward carrying a stout derrick. Its name arose from the puffing noise made by the early type of propelling machinery and the noisy exhaust from the steam winch – it was of 105–120 tons, with a length of 66ft (20m) and a draught, fully laden, of under 10ft, dimensions standardised to fit canal locks, for the craft were mostly built at Kirkintilloch, on the Forth and Clyde Canal a few miles north of Glasgow. In *Para Hardy and Other Tales*, which has become a humorous classic about the puffer, Neil Munro has captured the authentic atmosphere of island harbours, and even the speech and idiosyncrasies of the people there.

THE SEA ROADS

The nearest corner of the island to Oban is Auchnacraig, better referred to as Grass Point, on the south side of Loch Don, 7 miles from the mainland across the Firth of Lorne. Here in the old days converged not only the livestock of Mull, but also of Coll, Tiree, Morvern and Ardnamurchan.

A short but treacherous ferry crossed Loch na Keal between Gribun and Ulva or Torloisk, on the main north–south route for people moving between the Ross and the populous parish of Kilninian and Kilmore. This was the Ulva ferry that features in the poem by Thomas Campbell, when Lord Ullin's daughter (daughter of Sir Alan Maclean of Knock) was overwhelmed by a storm when eloping in the ferryboat with a young MacQuarrie chief to his island home in Ulva. No trace of the old Gribun ferry is to be seen today, and the modern Ulva ferry crossing is a stretch of water about three hundred yards wide between Ulva and the Torloisk–Salen road, with which it is connected by a half-mile side-road.

There was always a regular ferry between Iona and Fionnphort, which is now run by Caledonian-MacBrayne. From little piers at Carsaig, Croggan and Lochbuie there were sailings to Oban, Easdale and Crinan. In 1773 Dr Johnson and Boswell embarked at Lochbuie for Oban after their tour of Mull and Iona, and it was there that the formidable doctor was for once reduced to speechless indignation where the bluff laird of Lochbuie greeted him with: 'Are you of the Johnstones of Glencro or Ardnamurchan?'

A more regular pattern of routes began to emerge which was well established by the twentieth century. A daily mail-boat service ran between Tobermory and Oban, leaving Tobermory (where the boat tied up overnight) at about 7.30am, to shuttle between calling points on the Sound of Mull. The boat left Oban about 1pm (after the arrival of the mail-train from the South) for its return trip to Tobermory, making the same calls in reverse along the Sound of Mull.

Between 1 June and 30 September every year the popular Staffa and Iona steamer sailed from Oban, on a circuit of Mull, calling at Tobermory, Staffa and Iona. Then there was what was called the 'Islands' boat, based on Oban, sailing to Barra in the Outer Isles thrice weekly, calling at intermediate ports. This sailing still operates.

A large passenger-cargo boat run by MacBrayne sailed weekly from Glasgow, calling at Tobermory on its outward and inward trip to the Outer Isles. As a matter of interest, in 1892, the cost of the return trip from Glasgow to Stornoway, with a choice of detours, was between £6 and £7 for first-class passengers! This sailing competed with a sailing by McCallum Orme's two ships *Hebrides* and *Hebridean*, which called at Bunessan as well as at Tobermory. (The company amalgamated with MacBrayne between the wars.) There were also casual sailings by smaller cargo boats serving Lochbuie, Bunessan, Ulva, Tobermory and other ports round Mull, while in summer occasional excursions were run from Oban, as well as special runs for collecting wool, sheep and cattle.

Nowadays MacBrayne runs a regular service between Tobermory and Kilchoan. There are short excursions by private boats from Tobermory and elsewhere along the sea-lochs, and from Croig, Ulva Ferry and Bunessan/Fionnphort to the Treshnish Islands and west central Mull. The old ferry still runs from Grass Point catering for small cargoes and special runs.

The two main piers are at Tobermory and Craignure. Salen

pier was built originally by a private company, the Salen (Mull) Pier Company Limited. The present structure, is the third to have been built. Adverse winds and currents led to the abandonment of the first two. There are also piers at Calgary, Bunessan, Carsaig, Lochbuie and Grass Point, with smaller slipways at Croggan, Kintra, Ulva Ferry, Croig, Iona, Fionnphort and elsewhere. There are three piers at Tobermory; the small estate pier at Aros; the 'Old Pier' built before 1800, which can handle only small craft and is now owned by the local fishing association; and the 'New Pier' built by MacBrayne in 1864 and extended in the 1930s. An older slipway at the mouth of the Tobermory Burn was lengthened in the 1980s, but is of little practical use. After World War II the New Pier was allowed to fall into disrepair by the owners and ships had to lie off and land passengers by small boats. After strong protests to MacBrayne and the Secretary of State consent was given in 1984 to its restoration, at a cost of about £300,000, which was completed a year later.

MACBRAYNE AND THEIR SHIPS

It was Neil Munro who said that he was over twenty years of age before he realised that not all ships in the world had red funnels! The familiar black hulls, white upperworks and red funnels of the MacBrayne fleet stand for well over a hundred years of transportation in the face of geographical and increasing economical difficulties.

The first steamship to appear in the Mull area was the famous *Comet*, designed by Henry Bell, which began to sail between Greenock and Fort William in 1812. Steamship companies were soon formed. For instance, in 1836 the *Tobermory*, a wooden paddle-steamer of 80 tons, was built for 'a body of enterprising gentlemen consisting of landed proprietors, tacksmen, and merchants connected with Mull, Morvern and Ardnamurchan'. Two years later the sailing of the *Glen Albyn*, of 200 tons, was sponsored by the Glen Albyn Steamboat Company of Tobermory, a group of merchants and landowners in the district.

In July 1838, the *Rob Roy* began to sail from Oban to Staffa and Iona every Tuesday and Friday, returning on the evening following. In 1855 regular summer sailings on this run – which has been one of the most popular in Europe ever since – were inaugurated, have continued to the present day. After Queen Victoria included the Highlands and Islands in her Grand Tour of 1847 there followed an unprecedented expansion in the tourist trade of the area.

The year 1880 was a turning-point, for the Caledonian Railway was extended from Callander to Oban. Mull and the Hebrides were now in touch with Glasgow and the Lowlands at speeds hitherto unknown. Oban became known as the 'Charing Cross of the Highlands', and Mull, shared something of the new order.

Two developments followed: first, MacBrayne received the whole of the mail contract for the Western Isles; and second, in 1881 a daily mail-boat service was inaugurated between Tobermory and Oban which was to continue until 1964. Mull people agree that the daily Sound of Mull run between Tobermory and Oban was the sailing that has left the most nostalgic memories. They recall the delays on the days of the Oban markets, when sheep were given priority over passengers, and the Glasgow train might be caught with only minutes to spare. They remember sharing the already limited and uncomfortable passenger space with a packed woolly cargo of over 1,200 sheep, damp, smelly, and filling the air with their protests. The shepherds who accompanied them were dressed for the occasion in blue suits and black boots, hazel sticks in their fists, raincoats slung over their shoulders on a piece of rope; their collie dogs swarming at their heels, issuing protesting howls when accidentally trodden upon. Loading against time at every port of call, captain and mate were everywhere, screaming imprecations in the Gaelic. It always seemed to be raining at the time, with a half-gale blowing up the Firth of Lorne meeting the tide rip off Lismore lighthouse. Conditions 'tween-decks in the mixed aroma of sheep, kippers frying in the galley, and diesel oil may well be imagined!

The Pioneer, a paddle-steamer of 200 tons, was the first boat to take up this regular run in 1881 followed in 1893 by the

Carabineer, of 299 tons, also a paddle-steamer.

In 1908 the *Lochinvar*, a motor vessel of 216 tons, succeeded the *Carabineer*, and continued to run until 1955. She took about 3½ hours to cover the 30 miles between Tobermory and Oban.

In spite of criticisms of the scanty accommodation provided for passengers, who were separated into 'cabin' and 'steerage' classes, the *Lochinvar* gave dependable service over the years. There was one occasion in the 1920s when she aroused the anxiety of the whole Mull community. Held up in Oban one winter afternoon by a howling gale raging up the Firth from the open Atlantic, she ventured out at last during a short lull. Caught in the open by darkness and a fresh onset of the storm, and unable either to carry on or to return, she was obliged to turn tail to the wind, and vanished into the maze of islands, narrows and sea-lochs of Loch Linnhe. She somehow passed through, over or under the obstacles, and dropped anchor at last in unknown but sheltered waters. At daybreak she found herself anchored almost off Fort William, 30 miles north of Oban. There was relief and jubilation on Mull when she was reported safe, manned as she was by a crew hailing chiefly from Tobermory.

A few years later, in a thick fog, she cut clean through a fishing boat which had incautiously anchored off Craignure, fortunately with no loss of life. The mail-boat herself was little the worse for this encounter, and escaped serious damage again on another occasion when she collided with and sank another boat during a thick fog in Oban Bay.

Replaced by the *Lochearn* in 1955, the *Lochinvar* served as a relief ship based on Oban. She was sold to a company operating in the Thames Estuary and left Tobermory for good after a farewell run on 28 May 1960. In 1966 she was sailing north to take up duties as a cruise ship between Inverness and Invergordon. On the way, however, the fifty-eight-years-old ship was caught too close to a lee shore in a North Sea gale and was wrecked, with all hands lost, at Donna Nook, south of the Humber. Her bell, binnacle and steering-wheel are now kept at Duart Castle.

The *Columba*, 1,460 tons, service speed 14½ knots, designed to carry 600 passengers (400 in winter) and 60 motor cars, took up the new Craignure to Oban run in 1964, when the old Tobermory to Oban run was discontinued. She now operates on various other runs and in her place different boats serve the Craignure run.

The ship that served with most distinction was the *King George V*, of 900 tons. She took over the Staffa and Iona run in 1936, and was one of the twelve MacBrayne ships called up for war service between 1939 and 1945. When acting as tender on the Clyde, her duties were interrupted by the evacuation of Dunkirk. She made no fewer than six trips to and from the beaches in 1940, narrowly escaping air attacks and shellfire. Capt. Robert MacLean and Chief Engineer W. MacGregor were each awarded the DSO, and bo'sun D. J. MacKinnon the DSM.

The two world wars cost David MacBrayne Ltd dear in inflated running costs and overheads. In fact, without government intervention and subsidies the company could not have carried on. The Revenue Support Grant of £600,000 granted in 1969 had to be increased to £7.4 million for 1986. New ships had to be built to replace obsolete units. The government stepped in, built the ships, registered them in name of the Secretary of State for Scotland at the Port of Leith, and leased them to the company on long-term charter. However, the travelling public always regards them as MacBrayne ships in the old tradition.

The company, described by Magnus Magnusson as 'a legendary scapegoat of island ills', has a difficult problem. Its ships have to be economical in size to enable them to handle such a diversity of small consignments, and to call at so many places where shallow draught is essential. Tonnage (unless for specialised purposes, such as car-ferries) cannot exceed 1,000 tons and a 10ft 6in (3.2m) draught is about the limit. The company owns Tobermory, Lochaline and other piers, but elsewhere dues are payable to privately owned piers, adding to operating costs. The tourist season is short and dependent on the weather.

In 1969, Coast Lines Limited, who had in 1928 acquired a 50 per cent shareholding in MacBrayne, sold its interest to the

Scottish Transport Group, which already held the balance of the MacBrayne shares. The Group now owns this old company in its entirety. The company now operates under the title of Caledonian-MacBrayne, or 'Cal-Mac' for short.

CRAIGNURE PIER AND THE FUTURE

Prior to 1964 passengers and goods arriving at Craignure for the south of Mull had to be ferried in small boats in all weathers between the old slipway and the daily mail-boat. As far back as 1865 strong recommendations were being made that an adequate pier be built, but it was not until 1962, a hundred years later, that Argyll County Council decided to allow a modern pier to be built at Craignure to coincide with the introduction of a car-ferry. Thanks to a generous gift of £50,000 from the late Neil Cameron, of Tobermory, the project was completed even earlier than programmed, and in 1964 a modern structure was opened designed to handle motor cars from the new ferries operating on the roll-on roll-off principle. It was then the only such pier in the Hebrides and was to revolutionise transport to and from Mull.

The daily mail-boat was discontinued and in its place the car-ferry based on Oban provided Monday–Saturday return services to Craignure, up to six in summer and two in winter, with a Sunday service in summer, taking about forty-five minutes for the crossing, each way. Then in 1973 a ferry was opened between the slipways at Fishnish (off the main Salen–Craignure road) and Lochaline, in Morvern, with regular sailings throughout the day over the fifteen-minute crossing. It proved to be such a convenient link in the journey to or from Fort William and the north that in 1986 the earlier ferry, which could carry only six motor cars, was replaced by *The Isle of Cumbrae*, which, with three times the previous vessels' capacity, can also accommodate coaches. Caledonian-MacBrayne also issued a new ticket enabling vehicles and passengers to travel to Mull via Craignure and return to the mainland via Fisnish–Lochaline. The mile-long approach road through the Fishnish forestry plantations was suitably upgraded.

The ferry between Tobermory and Kilchoan in Ardnamurchan is a great convenience for the people of Ardnamurchan and also provides a useful tourist attraction, with several runs per day. It has been under threat of closure for the last year or two, but is continued meantime in response to strong public demand. Without it people in Ardnamurchan would have to travel over 30 miles to Fort William for their shopping instead of making this short crossing to Tobermory.

From Craignure Pier motor coaches convey passengers north to Salen and Tobermory and south to Bunessan and the Iona Ferry. Passenger fares compare unfavourably with a journey by rail in the Lowlands of almost exactly the same distance as Tobermory to Oban (30 miles).

Since the opening of the Oban Craignure car-ferry in 1964 there have been dramatic changes in the numbers of passengers and motor cars to and from the island during the summer season. The availability of convenient car transport to the island gives greater daily or short-time mobility to the islanders, attracts more visitors (and thereby creates new internal problems concerned with roads and accommodation) and, through stimulating greater interest in the island, brings more passengers to the mainland ferry termini of Oban and Lochaline.

Before the building of the new pier the drivers of motor cars leaving or landing on Mull had the hair-raising experience of driving from the level of the piers at Tobermory, Salen or Oban on to the congested upper deck of the daily mail-boat across two narrow planks tilted up or down according to the state of the tide. Later, cars were wrapped in a padded wide-mesh net and slung on board by the ship's derrick. Such methods were slow, and the number of cars few, limited in any case by the small deck space.

An analysis of the car and passenger traffic over the years appears later under 'The Tourist Industry.' Compare this with the more detailed tables that follow, showing figures for the last seven years on each of Mull's ferries:

	OBAN–CRAIGNURE			FISHNISH–LOCHALINE		
		Vehicles			*Vehicles*	
Year	*Passengers*	*Private*	*Commercial*	*Passengers*	*Private*	*Commercial*
1979	305,060	40,438	4,959	36,234	16,088	671
1980	280,241	39,072	4,522	38,372	15,820	431
1981	264,471	37,274	4,493	37,328	15,598	362
1982	271,792	39,829	4,466	35,901	15,514	352
1983	306,171	44,487	4,137	39,211	16,948	549
1984	338,802	49,559	4,311	42,720	19,190	434
1985	343,567	51,906	4,600	43,224	19,696	288

	FIONNPHORT–IONA		TOBERMORY–MINGARY	
			(Kilchoan)	
1979	156,854	Vehicular traffic	5,758	No vehicles
1980	157,552	negligible	6,259	
1981	156,772		4,217	
1982	151,860		5,189	
1983	157,876		5,233	
1984	169,180		6,345	
1985	178,150		5,733	

Charges for conveying motor cars are based on length. In 1969 the return charge on the Craignure–Oban ferry for a car of 12½ft (3.8m) was about £6. The same length of car in 1986 costs £19.40 to transport. There are substantial concessions for six-journey books of tickets (three return journeys), a concession which also applies to passenger fares. Commercial vehicles are charged at the rate of £2.70 per half metre (19½in) (plus VAT – 1986 rates), laden or unladen. Extra-wide vehicles pay 50 per cent extra. In 1979 a 9m (29ft 6in) lorry cost £39.60 (Oban–Craignure) or £28.80 (Lochaline–Fishnish). In 1986 boxes of salmon etc were conveyed from Tobermory to Oban (30 miles) at a cost of £4.27 per hundredweight (50kg) but from Oban to Glasgow at £5.64 per hundredweight, which is only £1.37 extra for the much longer haul of 110 miles from Oban to Glasgow.

A significant reduction in these costs would transform the economy of Mull. The question of introducing RET (Road Equivalent Tariff) – the equating of ferry charges to the running costs of a vehicle (petrol and oil, wear and tear) over the same distance was discussed and approved by an earlier government. Sadly, this worthwhile gesture to the islands was turned down in 1984. For example, the two costs quoted above would have been reduced from £39.60 to £3.93 and £28.80 to £1.37. Some such concession is long overdue in an island where the cost of living is estimated to be 20 per cent above that of the mainland. Without it no new commercial venture can hope to compete with the products of the mainland.

However desirable it would be to introduce competition in the services to the Western Isles, the result might well be to cream off the most profitable and risk the withdrawal of unprofitable runs, leading to the semi-isolation of some island communities and the collapse of their economy, and renewed depopulation in parts of the Western Isles.

After 1964 Cal-Mac organised a distribution system of lorries to handle goods from the mainland amounting to 120 tons weekly at the summer peak, 40 tons in the off-season. The 8 and 12 ton restrictions placed on many side-roads in Mull is a considerable handicap, confining heavy loads to the main Tobermory–Craignure–Fionnphort road and preventing the carriage of economic loads across the island. Tobermory Pier is still the company's storage centre on Mull, although its location in the extreme north adds to delivery distances and handling costs.

PLEASURE SAILINGS

The Craignure car-ferry offers a pleasant cruise from Oban for visitors. There are attractive local pleasure sailings. At Tobermory, cruises lasting from an hour or two to a whole day, depending on weather and choice of route, can be arranged. One popular outing is along Loch Sunart, the long, sheltered, picturesque sea-loch whose entrance lies between Morvern and Ardnamurchan opposite Tobermory Bay. Another enjoyable trip is round the cliffs of north and west Mull towards the open sea, with the blue outlines of the distant Hebridean islands standing out on the horizon. Here lie the fascinating Treshnish Islands, a bird and seal sanctuary, and Staffa, the pillared island, where landings are made if weather permits. The west of Mull can be explored by pleasure cruises from Croig, Ulva Ferry, Quinish and Bunessan/Fionnphort, while Grass Point is a centre for Loch Linnhe, the Firth of Lorne and the east of Mull. Small boats can be hired at most of these places for short private outings.

YACHTING

The Hebrides and west coast of Scotland are a paradise for the yachter – or, when the weather blows up, the reverse! In fine, clear sailing weather, with a fresh north-westerly wind, nothing can be more invigorating than the whip of the keen salty air, the sense of effortless speed and the long lift of the rollers whose reach extends far beyond the limits of the Hebrides, all backed by the extraordinary colours of sea and sky. However, in stormy weather, this is no place for the inexperienced. By keeping to the lee of the islands and following sheltered channels such as the Sound of Mull, a great deal of safe and enjoyable sailing can be done.

There are many well-charted anchorages round Mull. Care must be taken to study wind directions, for a sudden change can convert an apparently safe anchorage into a highly dangerous one. One favourite bay is the Bullhole, half a mile north of Fionnphort, which besides being safe is central for visiting the attractions of Iona. Another excellent spot is Loch na Lathaich, Bunessan. Neil Gunn's book *Off in a Boat* describes conditions around Mull from the angle of a small party cruising in an old motor-boat. Loch Tuath, at Ulva Ferry, Gometra island, Loch Spelve in the south, are all good, but Tobermory is the perfect centre, offering a welcome return to civilised amenities from beer to baths for crews who have perhaps been living for days under difficult conditions. Fifty or sixty yachts and cabin cruisers can be seen in the bay any day in July and August when the weather is fine. In such ideal circumstances it was inevitable that a local yacht club should come into being.

The Western Isles Yacht Club celebrated its Golden Jubilee in 1986. Children especially are attracted to the sport and every encouragement is being given to their training. The

Club runs a regatta every August. This was a local fixture started in the early 1900s, before the Yacht Club formally took over its organisation and widened its scope. It also shares with the two Oban clubs the running of the West Highland Yachting Week. One of the highlights of the yachting calendar is the exciting annual race from the Clyde to Tobermory in mid-July.

In 1982 a few enthusiasts formed a Sub-Aqua section within the Yacht Club. By 1986 this had expanded to a point where it was decided to form an independent organisation, but still affiliated to the Yacht Club, and a 5m semi-rigid hull boat has been purchased to allow access to various sites round the island.

The popularity of Tobermory Bay as a yachting centre has led to frequent congestion when the increasing number of yachts seek anchorages. In 1986, with the consent of the Crown State Commissioners, the local Tobermory Harbour and Fairways Council, was set up to control the allocation of moorings.

THE LIFEBOAT SERVICE

A lifeboat was stationed at Tobermory between 1937 and the late 1940s. It was manned by a volunteer crew with a full-time engineer. The boat was named the *Sir Arthur Rose* and gifted in his memory by the late Miss Lithgow, of Glengorm. However, the boat was withdrawn for it was stationed rather far from the area of potential danger and its services were rarely required. The lifeboats stationed at Port Askaig, (Islay), Mallaig, Barra Head and Oban now cover the area. There is a representative of the Coastguard Service stationed at Tobermory.

7   COMMUNICATIONS WITHIN THE ISLAND

U ntil almost the end of the eighteenth century roads in Mull were no more than rough ridge tracks and footpaths, and by the cattle-droving routes. Without wheeled vehicles the method of transport of goods was by creels or panniers carried on the backs of the islanders themselves, or slung across the tough little garrons, the Mull ponies which were smaller than their counterparts on the mainland and could carry no more than 1½cwt (76kg). The garrons were sometimes harnessed to light wooden sledges for such work as dragging stones off cultivated ground; the sledges might be forked tree branches or rough planks, rather like the American Indian *travois*.

When the spoked wheel came into use, rough tracks were formed for the passage of carts, which were at first no more than rough boxes on wheels. These demanded a heavier breed of horse, and by the end of the nineteenth century, with more and better roads and new farming methods, there were heavy draught horses for agricultural work, garrons for hill work (as on the sporting estates), and medium breeds for drawing passenger vehicles.

The people used the gig, or dog-cart, holding up to three passengers. The heavier hiring vehicle, with more comfort, was the 'machine' or wagonette, carrying seven or eight, drawn by one or two horses. On the steepest hills passengers were often obliged to alight and walk to the summit to ease the load for the horses; indeed the short-cuts used by the walkers can still be traced across many of the acute bends. Large troughs, filled by a seepage of bog water, were sited at the summits of many of the steep hills where the horses could have a drink and a rest. A few of these are still in position. Another

Page 105: (above) Ruins of Aros Castle, from a picture made about 1800 (Collection of A.D. Brown); (below) Duart Castle, stronghold of the Macleans of Duart

Page 106: (*left*) Kilmore Church, Dervaig, with unique pencil steeple; (*below*) Moy Castle, Lochbuie, former stronghold of the Clan MacLaine

useful small commercial vehicle was the spring cart of the delivery type with low sides, much used by travelling salesmen and tinkers.

DROVE ROADS

Old grassy tracks marking former lines of communication can be seen crossing the moorlands. Some of them end at peat banks, where the fuel was once dug to be carted home, but others pick their way across a saddle of the hills into the next valley. They all connect with old ruins and former townships and usually merge somewhere into the modern road system.

Many of these tracks were drove roads. Cattle landed at Croig were driven via Dervaig and Glenaros to Salen. At Druimtighe, at the head of Glenaros, other tracks came in from the glen above Kengharair Farm leading over to Torloisk and Treshnish. Salen was the focal point also for the drove road from Tobermory and district and for stock ferried over from Ardnamurchan. Thence the track continued to Craignure and Grass Point. Glen Forsa added its quota, and a main drove road began at Kintra, at the tip of the Ross of Mull, another landing-place for cattle. It traversed the Ross of Mull and after passing through Glen More it was joined by a track from Lochbuie, continuing to Grass Point.

At Salen, fairs, games and markets were held at seasonable times and are perpetuated to this day by the Mull and Morvern Agricultural Show, established in 1832 and held every August.

From Grass Point the cattle were shipped over to the island of Kerrera at Oban, landed there at the stone jetty in Barr nam Boc Bay on the western shore and driven across the island to the east side, and ferried across the narrow channel to the mainland about a mile south of the town of Oban. Sometimes they were secured by a length of rope to the stern of the boat and crossed partly swimming, partly towed. Here they were at the start of their long journey to the markets of the South by the network of mainland drove roads.

ROAD DEVELOPMENT

At the beginning of the nineteenth century the only road in Mull capable of taking a two-wheeled vehicle followed the coast between Salen and Grass Point. In 1790 the Duke of Argyll contributed £350 towards the making of this road. By 1807 it has been extended to Tobermory in the north and Lochbuie in the south, and it was about this time that a stagecoach was brought over to the island to prove that the road was indeed passable. The vehicle was taken back to the mainland immediately after this exacting experiment. Road construction on Mull lagged behind that on the mainland. In 1773 Dr Johnson hired horses to carry him by tracks and bridle-paths the 20 miles from Tobermory to Inch Kenneth, a route on which the rivulets, to which Boswell referred, could, in times of heavy rain, turn into swollen torrents, unbridged and dangerous to cross.

Up to 1840 there was very little expansion in the road system. The *Statistical Account* of 1845 criticised it severely; the roads, it said, 'are extremely bad and the improvement proceeds but slowly – the funds allowed are so dispropor-tionate to the extent and surface and to the expense requisite that unless aid from the government is obtained to assist proprietors in their laudable exertions to benefit the com-munity in opening up new lines and repairing the old, there is no hope of anything of an improvement for many years to come'. At the beginning of that decade a road was extended from Grass Point through Glen More as far as Kilfinichen, on the northern shore of Loch Scridain, linking the populous west-central part of Mull with the eastern area, giving greater access to the fairs and markets of Salen and Grass Point. An important bridle-path – it may even have taken carts at one time – led from Salen via Loch Ba across the southern ridge of Mam Chlachaig on the shoulder of Ben More, descending to Glen More near Kinloch. A branch of this path continued past the head of Loch Ba, up Glen Cannel, and across the ridge towards the eastern end of Glen More. 'Robertson's Pass' was a short cut from Grass Point across to Glen Forsa.

The natural expansion of the road through Glen More to

Bunessan and Fionnphort and elsewhere followed within ten years. Fortuitously enough, once the Clearances began there was no lack of cheap labour. For many able-bodied people, work on the roads removed the threat of abject poverty.

Before the days of bituminised surfacing the job of the roadman was quite specialised. He was something of a craftsman – wise in the selection of hammers of the exact length and weight for the job of preparing road metal – and something of a practical geologist too, for he had to assess the correct texture of the rocks he prised out of the quarries by the roadside to be split and broken down into smaller blocks. Those in turn were knapped down into specified sizes. Wages were paid on a piece-work basis. The expert roadman has disappeared from the rural scene and his work is now performed by machinery. We can no longer watch him, wearing his dark protective eye-shields and scuffed heavy boots, chipping away all day with a minimum of effort, adjusting his strokes to the texture and cleavage planes of the rocks.

Motor cars first appeared in about 1909, introduced by one or two of the landowners, and clouds of choking dust marked their passing in dry weather. The steep hills, acute bends and numerous hump-backed bridges demanded robustness rather than speed. One could outpace those early chain-driven Albions as they ground their way up the steeper hills, and if he was daring, a lad could (unknown to the driver) swing on behind one of the square vans and enjoy an exciting, if precarious, lift home. Besides the Albion, the Model T Ford was popular, and its simplicity and reliability introduced a new conception of transport to the public in Mull, as elsewhere. Other makes appeared, such as the Argyll, with its design in advance of the times, and exotic makes belonging to the lairds such as the Delaunay-Belville and Minerva.

MODERN ROADS

Mull has no lack of materials for road works. There are small grass-grown quarries every few hundred yards along the road-sides where the road-makers used to work. Some quarries supplied the hard whinstone, others the softer 'rotten rock' used to bind the sharp surfacing, the whole being levelled and consolidated first by the horse-drawn road-roller, then by the wheels of passing traffic.

The increasing use of motor cars demanded more and better roads. In Mull bituminised surfaces were introduced in the 1930s, bringing to an end the dust and irregularities in the surface. Specially prepared surfacing material is now brought in to convenient piers by small coasters from mainland dumps, such as Loch Etive, north of Oban, in loads of up to 300 tons. This is distributed by motor lorry to the various road gangs throughout the island.

Strathclyde Region is now responsible for the upkeep of 144 miles of classified roads in Mull, including a few short stretches within the Tobermory township, and 2½ miles in Iona. The only Class I road is the 49 mile coast road from Tobermory via Craignure and Glen More to Fionnphort. The section from Tobermory to Salen is still substandard, but the remaining length has many miles of excellent modern road construction, although mostly single tracked, with passing places. There are about 51 miles of Class II roads and 34 of Class III. The Forestry Commission is increasingly building lengths of private road; others have been constructed by the Department of Agriculture and handed over to Strathclyde Region for maintenance.

Over twenty years ago the amount of traffic recorded just failed to reach a figure that would justify the construction of two-track roads. As the car-ferry statistics show, more recent figures prove the urgent need for such roads. If the tourist industry continues to expand, and brings with it a still greater increase in road traffic, many side-roads will prove quite inadequate during the summer season. In the summer, on the popular Tobermory to Calgary second-class road, there have frequently been as many as half a dozen cars queued up at passing places to allow oncoming cars to proceed. Some of the out-of-date narrow bridges have been damaged by long commercial vehicles. Visibility at corners should be improved by cutting back encroaching scrub and bracken; as it is, the innumerable dry-skid marks on road surfaces bear witness to emergency stops by impatient or frustrated drivers; and of course, the island people are delayed in going about their business. Currently, much-needed employment would be provided in a road reconstruction programme and something of lasting value provided for the economy. In any case, it will be imperative to have a new road programme when the forests reach maturity and heavy loads of timber have to be conveyed.

The figure for cars in Mull can only be estimated. Personal observation suggests that in 1969 there must have been at least 300 motor vehicles regularly in use in Mull, including private, agricultural, forestry, goods, passenger and postal vehicles, and a small number of motor cycles – a ratio of about one vehicle to seven of the population. By 1986 there was a considerable increase in the number of vehicles. In contrast there are only half a dozen or so motor vehicles in Iona. However, it is unfortunate that restrictions on the landing of cars on the island have been relaxed. There is more than ample parking space at the Mull ferry terminus for the cars of visitors to Iona.

Although narrow and hilly, with many dangerous corners, weak culverts and narrow bridges, the roads are well surfaced. Lacking proper foundations the roads develop sudden dips and undulations over the many soft peaty stretches, and although these are a deterrent to speeding they are too often a danger to heavily laden vehicles, thus requiring the imposition of a maximum weight limit of 8–12 tons.

However, it is true that passing places and lay-bys are being slowly extended, and sight-lines improved at some blind corners. The spectacular alternative road from Salen to Fionnphort by Gribun, (9 miles longer,) winds for nearly a mile under the 1,000ft (305m) crumbling cliffs, cutting in places through the solid rock, with unprotected drops to the sea. The area is subject to land-slipping, very often started by a sheep dislodging a stone far up the steep slopes, which starts off a miniature avalanche. This is particularly so after periods of frost or heavy rain. On one occasion a postal van was immobilised for days when one rock-fall came down just in front of it, and before the postman could reverse another came crashing down behind him, effectively cutting off the van.

Forestry roads play their part in general communications, such as the service road branching off the main Tobermory–Salen road a mile above Aros Bridge, cutting through the woodlands to Loch Frisa and Lettermore. One old public road extensively used in past days ran from Dervaig to Glengorm, which has only the one road linking it with Tobermory. This has been taken over as a forestry service road. Plans were made some years ago to use this road – which is reasonably straight and level – and link it up with Glengorm and the Tobermory–Dervaig road just west of the Mishnish Lochs, thus cutting out the steep winding ascent from Dervaig and descent to Achnadrish.

As a result of constant gear-changing, slowing, stopping and starting, a motorist will find his petrol consumption increasing by about 20 per cent. Furthermore, the price of petrol is about 10p higher than on the mainland. There is a clear case for government relaxation of the level of VAT or petrol duty for all the islands, perhaps keeping the total cost of petrol to the driver on a level with that at the nearest point of the mainland – Oban in the case of Mull. The motor vehicle is such an essential item in the social and business economy that the benefits of this comparatively small subsidy would be apparent in some reduction in the cost of living.

In 1968 Mull was chosen as a venue for the annual rally run by the 2300 Motor Car Club of Blackburn. With the co-operation of the local police, livestock-owners and the public, this rally has taken place every year since then, during the first week of October, attracting up to 130 cars driven by some of the best drivers in Britain. The event attracts a large number of visitors, providing valuable publicity for the island and a late boost to the tourist trade in the north of Mull. It is estimated that 75 per cent of the visitors attending the rally return to Mull for a holiday.

By and large, Mull is a place where – subject to considerate driving – a motorist can relax. There are no double yellow lines, no parking meters, no traffic lights and only a few white guiding lines in the whole system. Some of the side roads still have a line of grass, or worn-down oily rushes, along the centre of the road, reminding the motorist that he or she is indeed far from mainland speed tracks. However, caution and concentration are demanded from drivers. Early cars could average no more than 12–15mph in Mull. On the slowly improving side-roads the modern car can average 25–30mph safely. For strangers accustomed to fast mainland driving, the roads can be frustrating, or even hazardous. On the unfenced sections the motorist must constantly be watchful for cattle and sheep, which can move quickly and unpredictably out of bushes or thick bracken. In spring, especially, lambs and their mothers can be a real hazard. Loss of animals caused by selfish or unfortunate drivers brings financial loss to crofters dependent on livestock for a living. Sadly accidents involving impacts are not uncommon.

PUBLIC TRANSPORT

Mull is not well served by public transport, though without it the island community cannot function effectively – another argument in favour of government concessions for island vehicles. Apart from MacBrayne's bus service from Craignure to Tobermory and Fionnphort, one or two private contractors and several vans running on Post Office private contracts, travellers have to make their own transport arrangements.

Minibuses are used to convey pupils from scattered homes to and from school. These vehicles could be integrated into a more general service for the travelling public. In addition, the suggestion could be followed up of using Post Office vehicles for carrying fare-paying passengers, as well as for delivering parcels and light goods; passenger-carrying facilities already exist on the Tobermory–Dervaig–Calgary run.

In the tourist season MacBrayne and a few private hirers organise coach tours. A nucleus of this network might be retained during the off-season, using smaller buses with a more frequent service. Under present conditions, however, this could not be a paying proposition.

Mull, however, is the only island in the Hebrides to have its own passenger railway! This is a miniature railway of 10¼in gauge running for 1½ miles between Craignure and Torosay

Castle. The idea was the brainchild of Mr. Graham Ellis, of Salen, and for four years a small team of volunteers worked to survey, clear and level the ground, making a route through the woodlands for the permanent way. The rails were laid, engines and rolling stock acquired. Dependent at first on voluntary subscriptions, finances finally stabilised and the project was completed with a grant from the Highlands and Islands Development Board. The railway, known as the Mull and West Highland Narrow Gauge Railway Co Ltd, was officially opened in June 1984 and has already become a valuable tourist attraction and a unique link between Craignure and Torosay Castle, which attracts over 20,000 visitors during the season.

AIR TRANSPORT

An air landing strip is situated at the mouth of Glen Forsa, on the Sound of Mull, 2 miles east of Salen and not far from the hospital and old people's home there. Opened for regular flights by Loganair on 13 September 1966, it was built as an exercise by the sappers of the 38th Engineer Regiment on behalf of the then Argyll County Council, in fifty-four days, at a cost stated to have been £6,000, a fraction of what it would have cost as a commercial venture. The runway is grass over gravel, 3,000ft (915m) long by 90ft (27m) wide, and the work of levelling involved moving 50,000 tons of earth and clearing away 1,000 trees. The airstrip is only 30 minutes' flight from Glasgow Airport via Ganavan, beside Oban, which is only 5 minutes' flight distant. The record time taken for a flight from Mull to Glasgow Airport was 22 minutes; from Mull to London Airport (changing planes at Glasgow), just under two hours.

The airstrip was used for a few years for regular flights to Glasgow by Loganair, but that service was discontinued, and the airstrip is now used only by the occasional private aeroplane.

COMMUNICATIONS WITHIN THE ISLAND

On his visit to Mull Dr Johnson was on tenterhooks at the idea of missing a sailing boat that would carry his correspondence over to Easdale. In those days the conveyance of mail depended on fortuitous transport to and from the island.

The question of a post office was raised first in 1776 by the factor of the Duke of Argyll, but it was not until 1791 that a customs house and post office were set up in Tobermory. About 1801 a small packet-boat began to run between Croig and Tiree carrying passengers and letters every Thursday, weather permitting. The Post Office paid the Duke an annual subsidy of £5 for this service. Tenants of the Argyll estates in Mull were obliged to use this boat to transport their cattle and goods. The organisation of postal services within the island did not develop until the 1840s. MacBrayne received its first mail contract in 1852, but this may not have included the Mull district. In 1845 there was a thrice-weekly mail service between Grass Point and Oban, probably run by a private contractor.

Up to this time charges had been graduated according to a mileage chart based on London as the centre, but under the new regulations the Penny Post was set up for deliveries over any distance. Postage stamps had to be cancelled by an impression showing the identity, but not the name, of the office of posting. In Scotland this took the form of a heavy square of horizonal bars with a rectangular space in the centre which bore the national number of the office, each office being allocated a different number. Reference to early editions of the *London Post Office Directory* (1844–5) and later *Guides* (1856–7 onwards) shows when post offices were first opened in different parts of Mull. Their importance varied with the movements of population, improving transport and even the convenience of local lairds.

In 1883 the cancellation system was replaced by the composite double circle (the principle of our modern franking system) showing the name of the post office instead of the number.

Tobermory was the chief post office for Mull, Iona, Tiree

and Coll until November 1964. It has been reduced to a sub-office under Oban, which is now the chief office for the Mull district. In 1986 there were twelve sub-offices in the Mull area: Aros (Salen), Bunessan, Craignure, Dervaig, Fionnphort, Isle of Iona, Lochbuie, Loch Don (formerly Auchnacraig), Pennyghael, Tiroran, Tobermory and Ulva Ferry. Gribun post office closed on 31 January 1971 and Torloisk on 4 January 1974. Throughout the island there is generally one collection and one delivery daily, carried out by official mail-vans, motor cycles and private mail contractors. Mails now converge on Craignure and are carried by the car-ferry to Oban. In 1986 there were still two of the familiar red pillar boxes in Tobermory with the rare inscription 'Edward VIII'. Only a few of these were installed throughout the kingdom during his short reign.

Deliveries on Mull can be as complex as on the remote islands of the Hebrides. For instance, the farms at Tavool and Burg on the south side of the headland of Ardmeanach are isolated from the main road by a 5 mile track which crosses the high shoulder of the hill at fierce gradients and is liable to be cut by wash-outs after heavy rain. The mail for these farms travels the 19 miles by van through Glen More from Craignure to Pennyghael. From there the postman takes the road by Kilfinichen Church, delivering as he goes to isolated farms and houses, thence by the side-road to Tiroran, where he leaves the van. From here he walks up the rough track to the summit, where he used to keep a bicycle padlocked to a telephone pole (even distant Burg has a telephone). After 4 miles of walking and cycling he reaches the end of the road at Burg. Now that the road has been improved somewhat a motor cycle – or a robust car – can be substituted for the cycle.

The case of the postman at Burg cannot compare with that of his counterparts at the end of the nineteenth century, when mail from Oban – at least that for the south of Mull – was still being handled at Grass Point. At that time the postman covering the ground between Pennyghael and Grass Point lived at Salen. He began his round by walking the 3 miles to Knock, beside Loch Ba, then 7 miles up the side of the loch, over Mam Chlachaig across the shoulder of Ben More and down to the Glen More road east of Kinloch Inn. There he was met by the Ross of Mull postman, who had already walked from his home at Pennyghael to Bunessan to collect the outgoing mail and then all the way back to his meeting-place, a round journey of 26 miles, reversing the procedure with incoming mails. The mail container the postmen were concerned with was hardly more than a foot square, containing the whole mail from the Ross of Mull.

Even when the letters on this route finally arrived at Bunessan they might lie for weeks in the little post office until someone living near the addressee happened to call, and agreed to hand in the letter at its destination.

At the Iona end of Mull, in the early days of the twentieth century the mails were delivered from Oban three times a week by the steamers *Fingal* and *Dirk*. From Iona the steamers continued to Fionnphort and Bunessan (where they tied up over night), Tiree, Coll, Tobermory, Salen, Craignure, and back to Oban. By that time, too, a horse-and-gig service ran between Craignure and Pennyghael.

When the parcel post was introduced, it offered a valuable shopping medium to the islanders. Few houses were without their catalogues from the city warehouses, and everything from trout flies to Sunday suits came by post. Commercial travellers were a common sight in Mull with their cases of samples. An echo from the old days is heard in a conversation between two local Tobermory men on the arrival of the daily mail-boat: 'Did anybody come on the boat today?' – 'Yes, two chentlemen, a cow and a commercial traveller.'

TELEGRAPH AND TELEPHONE SERVICES

Mull was first connected with the mainland by submarine telegraph in 1871, when a cable 6.4 nautical miles long was laid between Ganavan Bay (Oban) and Grass Point. This was connected on the island with telegraph offices at Tobermory, Dervaig, Calgary, Craignure, Pennyghael, Tiroran, Fionnphort, Bunessan and Iona. The new telegraph wires sang a strange and lonely note across the moorlands in the strong sea winds. On some of the grouse moors the wires were hung every few yards with squares of metal ('spectacles') about 6in (15cm) by 4in (10cm) pierced by two round holes, to warn off low-flying birds. This custom was discontinued long ago owing to the vast reduction in the number of game-birds; further, during World War II certain lines were transferred to underground conduits, starting with the Tobermory–Dervaig–Calgary section, and locally in Tobermory, Craignure and Dervaig.

The telegraph service was particularly appreciated by the merchants of the island; and in this connection a story has come down from the days of wartime restrictions and regulations. A butcher had just called at a Mull post office and sent off a telegram. After he had left, the postmistress turned to another local man who had just come in, and in that happy spirit which characterises certain confidential transactions in out-of-the-way places, she remarked, 'Now, isn't that a funny message to be sending to the suppliers in Oban: "Don't send meat – am killing myself!" ' The man pondered this seriously for a long time and then agreed, 'Yess, indeed; it iss a stupid message; I'm sure he knows fine he cannot be killing himself without a licence!'

The first telephone exchange was opened in Tobermory on 12 December 1931 with one call office and twelve private subscribers. At the same time an omnibus circuit was provided within the island connecting the post offices at Iona, Fionnphort, Bunessan and Pennyghael, while another connected Tobermory with Coll and Tiree, through Dervaig and Calgary. The cable to the islands dipped into the sea at Calgary Bay, connecting the circuit with Scarinish, Tiree, 25 miles distant. One Mull banker described the telephone as one of the most unfortunate services that ever came to the island: 'When I am trying to tide my customers over the winter with a loan or two, there is head office on the telephone calling me to question!'

In 1934 Mull was at last connected with the mainland by a submarine cable following the line of the former telegraph cable across to Oban. By the end of the 1960s the service had expanded to include 410 subscribers, with twenty public call-boxes and kiosks operating through eight telephone exchanges. The Iona exchange, opened in June 1935, served forty-four subscribers, with two public call offices. Even Gometra House, one of the remotest corners of Mull and its islands, was connected in 1958. The poles run from Ulva Ferry for 6 miles along the rough road through Ulva then over a narrow bridged channel of the sea, then a further mile across Gometra to the end of the line.

The linesmen in Mull are faced with many a difficult maintenance problem, especially when storms blow in unchecked from the Atlantic. In November 1966, one particularly fierce gust caught a road contractor's hut with two linesmen sheltering inside it, lifted it bodily into the air, and blew it into a bed of sixteen telephone wires. The poles here were 24ft (7.3m) above the ground, which adds a grain of truth to a statement made afterwards by one of the men that for the duration of the flight he had been affected by airsickness!

NEWSPAPERS, RADIO AND TELEVISION

Daily newspapers reach Mull (Craignure) with the first ferry of the day. The *Glasgow Herald* is probably the most popular for general and business information, with the *Scotsman* a close second. 'Hot' news is provided by the *Scottish Daily Express* or the *Daily Record*. Local and district news comes weekly in the *Oban Times*, which has been printed and published in Oban since 1861, and in the *People's Journal*, a weekly paper printed in Dundee, which provides more general news of the Highlands and Islands. Sunday newspapers reach Mull by Craignure in summer, or Grass Point when the Sunday ferry does not run. At the time of writing, the locally published monthly news magazine *Am Muileach* is proving quite popular.

As in the rest of the country, evenings are now spent far more frequently at home, watching television or listening to the radio. The quality of television reception is poor because of the shadowing effect of the big hills and the distances from relay stations, the nearest of which were Skye and Oban. However, a powerful relay station sited at Craignure and another at Glengorm have vastly improved reception. Never-

8 *SOCIAL CONDITIONS*

L ife in Mull can never have been easy over the centuries and it has become even more economically and socially complex. The islanders have had to face many frustrations and seeming injustices which have arisen both because their home *is* an island and because of their incorporation into a larger society that enjoys greater material advancement.

HOUSING

In Mull, where wood was scarce and stone abundant, buildings survived for a long time; hence Mull appears to have a very large number of settlements. From the seventeenth century, settlements began to be established all over the island. With the passage of time housing standards were slowly improved, but it was not until the second half of the nineteenth century that the more primitive types of houses were vacated, or rebuilt to improved standards.

The oldest type of house conformed to the general pattern adapted in the Hebrides. This type has very thick double walls, the central cavity being filled with dry peat and pebbles. The rafters, thin wooden tree-trunks, were stretched across the inner walls and angled to form a roof, which was thatched with barley straw, heather or turf, and held down with ropes of twisted heather weighted with stones. Rain ran off into the central cavities of the walls, the dampness keeping the infilling draughtproof. The stones forming the inner wall were laid with an outward tilt, and the general effect was to keep the interior warm, dry and draughtproof. In later buildings the rafters – known as cabers – were extended to cover the whole width of the walls.

While the remains of buildings of this type can be found in

121

many corners of Mull the deserted twin townships of Crakaig and Glac Gugairidh (The Hollow of the Dark Grazings), are typical examples. They lie in a sheltered hollow above the cliffs overlooking Loch Tuath, between Treshnish and Torloisk. Up to the middle of the nineteenth century they had a combined population of about two hundred, catered for by a blacksmith and other tradesmen. The last members of the dwindling community left just about the turn of the century. There is a large walled garden, presumably shared by the community as a whole and a sizeable sheep fank (fold). The houses were set down to no regular plan. They varied in size from 20ft (6m) by 12ft (3.7m) (interior measurements) to tiny cot-houses, all of them with walls 3ft (90cm) thick. They were built by craftsmen who used hardly any mortar except round the doors and windows. The mortar used was made from calcined seashells, hard and enduring, also to be seen in the window facings of the ancient ruined chapels, an art handed down from the days of monk-craftsmen. Houses had one door-way in the long side and up to four windows. Inside and out the surfaces of the walls were faced with stone blocks chipped to a uniformly smooth surface, and the outside corners were evenly rounded. The whole pattern was snug and streamlined, with a pathway of large flat stones laid round the outside walls. Water was obtained from a fast, clear-water burn flowing through the settlement.

One particular house style is believed to have been peculiar to Mull. It was built with one square and one round gable. Towards one gable-end an open tilted bucket-type chimney was built into the thatch; not so much a chimney (none of the houses had a built-in fireplace) as a vent through which the dense smoke escaped from the fire of peats kept burning all the time in the middle of the floor, which was of beaten earth, strewn with fresh straw, rushes or heather. Against the walls were low platforms covered with blankets over a foundation of springy heather tops, which served as beds; shelves were easily fitted into the stonework of the walls.

Below the permanent layer of smoke the air was reasonably clear, which accounts for the low-set design of seats and chairs used by earlier generations. Peat smoke was thought to be a fumigant which lessened the risk of disease. Domestic animals, the cattle and sheep, when sharing the same roof, entered the house by the one door and were separated from the occupants by a low partition, or simply tethered at the other end of the room which was built with a slight down-slope to allow for drainage. They helped to keep up the temperature in cold weather.

This way of life has been described by the Scottish expression 'the clartier (dirtier) the cosier!' But before one condemns old buildings like these as insanitary hovels, it must be remembered that outside lay the fresh open moorlands over which blew the cleansing sea winds, and the people were engaged in heavy, healthy work in the open air. These houses were in fact much superior to the contemporary miserable, congested and ill-ventilated slums of the Lowland cities – even to the seventeenth- and eighteenth-century houses of the nobility along the Royal Mile in Edinburgh.

The style of house described above is called a 'black house' today. It was originally so named not as a reflection on the appearance or sanitation, but to distinguish dry-stone walling from later styles of building. The expression *tigh dubh* (black house) is suggested by Dr Sinclair to have been correctly *tigh tughath*, (thatched house), the confusion having arisen through similarity of pronunciation.

Nowadays Argyll and Bute District Council is responsible for housing in Mull. In proportion to its size of population, the island's waiting list (68 in 1986) is high for Argyll, a fact doubtless accounted for by the number of people who would normally have left for jobs on the mainland which are no longer available. A high standard of building has been set throughout Mull, nearly always including full services, cleansing, sewers, electricity and mains water. Building costs are high; the council pays 40 per cent more for a standard council house in Mull than, say, in central Argyll, and nearly double the cost of a similar house in a Lowlands county such as Ayrshire. The number of residential caravans, especially around Tobermory and Bunessan, is an indication of housing needs. Repairs are very expensive, their cost often aggravated by the lack of skilled labour, especially for specialised work.

Although private builders find that pre-fabricated or timber-framed houses cost 25 to 60 per cent more than on the mainland, it is cheaper to use this type of construction rather than brick because of the high cost of bringing loads of bricks to Mull and the subsequent erection costs.

Private owners who want to build are at a disadvantage. Sites are hard to obtain, and costly. Many of these are located where services such as mains water and drainage are not available, though electricity is now much more accessible. The planning department is reluctant to allow building permission because of this, preferring that people should be herded into villages and towns where such services are available. This urbanisation in time will lead to still more deserted areas of the countryside, which is most undesirable.

Sanitary facilities in Mull, formerly non-existent in the settlements, are now standardised practically throughout the island, although a very few houses still have no running water laid on. Improvements and modernisation can be undertaken by an owner only at prohibitive cost (unless eligible for a grant towards the project) which would mean an exorbitant economic rent if the property were not owner-occupied. The price of houses has soared in recent years as a result of demands by non-residents for holiday accommodation. Moreover, residents with limited means can hardly afford to buy and restore houses for retirement in competition with in-comers investing in holiday accommodation. There are now (in the mid-1980s) at least three hundred holiday houses and second homes in Mull and Iona.

FUEL AND LIGHTING

Peat was of course the staple fuel, supplemented by coarse heather and any wood cast up on the shores or buried in the bogs. Care had to be taken in the appropriation of driftwood, for the ownership of timber cast up by the sea was vested in the Superior of the ground, as recorded in old records of the Argyll Estates. Coal was far too expensive for the ordinary people when it was first brought in by the early-nineteenth-century ships. It sold then at 10s to 12s per ton (50p to 60p).

Later, when coal came into more common use, it was delivered in loads from puffers. One cart-load of coal (approximately a ton) was equal to between twenty and forty loads of peat, depending on quality.

Mull peat does not have the same depth or high quality as the fine, hard black peat found in some of the other Hebridean islands, but it was adequate enough. Concessions were held by people in Iona and some neighbouring islands to cut peats over in Mull. The initial clearing of the surface was particularly tough, formed as it is by the matted roots of heather, bog-myrtle and coarse grasses. Below that the peats were cut with a spade of special design made by the local blacksmith. The peat blocks varied in size and shape in different regions. In Mull they were fairly standardised in blocks about 18in (46cm) in length by 4in (10cm) square, and they were cut at an angle of about 30° from the vertical.

A stockpile of peats, neatly stacked to allow the rain to run off, used to be a familiar site outside every cottage; an average household would burn about fifteen thousand peats a year, involving at least fifteen days' cutting, and countless days on the moors of turning and drying, for peat, when freshly cut, contains up to 95 per cent water.

Occasionally the bogs supplied roots of resinous bog-fir, the remains of ancient forests. Those, when dried and split, were used to light the houses, being held in iron sconces fixed into the walls, and also for kindling. Another form of lighting, which added to the miscellaneous odours, was provided by 'cruisies', or little iron containers, filled with fish- or seal-oil and fitted with a wick formed from the dry pith of rushes. All these iron implements (which are now sought as curios) were made by the local blacksmith or iron-worker.

The nostalgic tang of peat smoke is now rarely met; peats are cut in a few outlying districts. Paraffin oil lamps were succeeded by pressure types fitted with incandescent mantles which were used until electricity became available. In modern kitchens coal has often been replaced by oil, now that small oil-tankers can be transported on to the Mull roads. With the escalating price of oil, however, its popularity has fallen. Bottled gas is still used for heaters and small appliances.

SOCIAL CONDITIONS

Some of the larger houses, such as the estate mansion houses, used coal-gas generated on the premises and stored in a miniature gas-holder. In 1865 Torosay Castle used 14 tons of gas-coal in the year, priced at £1 per ton, and 60 tons of domestic coal at 11s to 13s (55p to 65p), part of which was a perquisite of some of the estate workers. Some houses used acetylene gas generated from calcium carbide. All these alternatives have now been superseded by electricity and oil, and the luxury of central heating is very much to the fore, especially in new houses. Some of the large isolated houses, such as Inch Kenneth House or Ulva House, used a paraffin-diesel generating plant to provide their own electricity.

FOOD AND DRINK

Up to the middle of the eighteenth century, when potatoes were introduced, the diet of the people was rather limited. Barley and oats of poor quality were grown and ground into a coarse meal with hand-querns, and later by water-mills. This meal was used for making bannocks and gruel, and thickening kail soup and similar dishes. Kail (a kind of cabbage) was the only green vegetable grown, at least up to the early nineteenth century, but it had a high vitamin C content that helped to balance the monotonous diet.

Fish – fresh, dried or salted – was an important item of diet, and the crofter-fishermen could always meet the needs of the maritime townships. Shellfish, too, must have been eaten in abundance, to judge from the quantity of shells found in old kitchen middens. Edible seaweeds, such as dulse and carragheen, were a healthy dish. The last named was made into a kind of blancmange by boiling it with milk.

Salmon traps were a common sight across the shallows at the mouths of burns and rivers where they entered the sea. The trap was a low, level dry-stone wall, built in curves to form little bays, which was deeply covered at high tide and left high and dry when the tide receded. Salmon and sea-trout, and also grey mullet, drifted over them towards the river mouth at high tide, and when the tide went out and the wall became exposed they were often trapped behind it and could be picked up at low tide. While the fish belonged to the local landowner, people naturally took any advantage they could of this easy presentation of food. One excellent example of a salmon trap can still be seen across the shallows of the estuary where the river Bellart enters the sea at Dervaig, in the north of Mull.

Meat was scarce, little more than the flesh of a goat or a braxy sheep (that is, one that died from natural causes not affecting the flesh). Beef was seldom seen: cattle were too valuable to be slaughtered for food, the best animals were exported and the poorest kept for breeding. In times of real food scarcity those animals were bled and the blood mixed with oatmeal to enrich and eke out the meagre store of food. Occasionally someone might kill a deer, or a wild-fowl, with the risk of being caught and dealt with by the landowners.

Sea-birds and their eggs were an important source of food. Young birds were captured in the early summer and salted down in barrels for winter use. Puffins and gannets (said to taste like salt beef) added to the menu, as did cormorants, which were edible after being buried for a few days in soft earth which absorbed the strong fishy taste.

It was not until about 1840 that the use of such luxuries as tea, sugar and wheaten bread became general, and of course by then potatoes were plentiful. The food was natural and unadulterated, with the whole grain retained and the vitamin content high. Evidence of this is seen in the tall stature and well-preserved teeth of that generation.

The drink of the ordinary people was, as elsewhere, ale. Wine was drunk only by the well-to-do. In Gaelic an inn is not a 'whisky-house' but an 'ale-house' – *Tigh leann*. The start of whisky distilling (in Ireland it is spelt 'whiskey') dates from the sixteenth century, and it became so widespread that the government stepped in and imposed an excise duty. A wave of illicit distilling swept the island and continued up to the early nineteenth century. In 1780 whisky sold for tenpence a quart (about 4p). Of course, the lairds and leading families could obtain ample supplies of luxuries like wines and silks, which were easily smuggled in among the islands and sea-lochs.

HEALTH

The islanders shared with the mainland folk the risks and incidence of the diseases of past centuries, though, apart from endemic diseases, the people were healthy, tall, active and of good physique. However, life was hard and exacting; child mortality was high and life expectation low by modern standards.

Severe outbreaks of smallpox, cholera and typhus occurred through ignorance of health principles and lack of hygiene. The incidence of tuberculosis was heavy until modern times, and the various forms of rheumatism were common.

The installation of proper sanitation came about slowly. In spite of the ample supplies of good fresh water available piped water was slow to be introduced. In fact, until comparatively recently, Mull was below the Scottish average, even below the standards of the county of Argyll, in the number of houses with mains water supply. It is related that in the early days of plumbing, one man who had proudly laid a sewer from his house was found, when moving to another house, to be lifting the drainage tiles, arguing that the sewer was part of the movable fittings!

Relatives returning home to Mull from distant places often carried infection that hit these isolated communities with particular virulence. Smallpox, especially, was regarded with almost superstitious horror, and the victims were sometimes completely isolated, food and drink being left where they could be collected. Volunteer nurses were few and far between and the sick were often left to die unattended. However, a different tale is told by a story from 1891, when – even at that late date – there was an outbreak of smallpox in the Ross of Mull. Shunned by neighbours, the occupants of the two houses involved were cared for by a complete stranger, a travelling pedlar, who nursed them through the illness. Resuming his rounds with his pack on his back, he found that he himself had contracted an attack of the disease so virulent that he died by the roadside. He was buried, along with his pack, on the spot where his body was found, a place now marked by a little cairn surmounted by a simple iron Celtic cross, beside the Pedlar's pool, as it is called, on the River Lussa in Strathcoil.

In the days when culture reached its highest standards covering a period of four hundred years from the fourteenth century onwards, a form of medical service was provided in the Hebrides by the Beatons, the famous Mull doctors, to whom fuller reference is made later. The art of medicine died out in Mull partly through the general decline in culture which followed the breakdown of the clan system, partly because of the specialised teaching and increasing skills in medicine that were developing in the Scottish Lowlands.

Mull is now within the scope of the National Health Service, which is administered by the Oban and District Hospital Board. There are three doctors, stationed at Tobermory, Salen and Bunessan, and until the facilties of a chemist became available recently in Tobermory, the doctors had to dispense most of their own prescriptions. There are six district nurses, based at Tobermory, Salen, Dervaig, Lochdonhead, Craignure and Bunessan. For dental treatment Mull people have to travel to the mainland, if they do not manage to see the visiting dentist.

The health authorities are faced with problems arising from the disproportionate number of elderly people who need specialised attention. A medical centre and home, known as Dunaros, was established at Salen in the early 1960s and proved to be so valuable that in five years it was upgraded to the status of a small hospital, and an X-ray unit was provided. There were then seven geriatric and five sick-bay beds, and since then the hospital has been extended still further.

There are arrangements in force allowing for the emergency deployment by day of an air ambulance using the Glen Forsa airstrip (2 miles distant), but night ambulance flights are not considered practicable because of the mountainous approach to the airstrip and the lack of basic ground-control equipment. Whether the travelling is done by official or private means, no emergency case is ever allowed to suffer undue delay in reaching specialised care on the mainland.

SOCIAL CONDITIONS

The need to provide publicly for the general welfare of the islanders arose only after the clan system had broken down. After the seventeenth century the island society might have been completely demoralised but for the steadying influence of the Church, acting through the Kirk Sessions. In fact, minor offenders against society were in greater fear of the wrath of the Kirk Sessions than are their more numerous modern counterparts of the courts of law.

Up to the time of the Reformation Mull was composed of a number of small parishes centred on the various churches. After the Reformation these were amalgamated into the single parish of Mull; but in 1688 the area north of Loch na Keal became the parish of Kilninian and Kilmore, the rest of Mull being the parish of Ross. Forty years later the Ross parish was subdivided into the two parishes of Torosay, and Kilfinichen and Kilviceon. Iona was decreed a *quod sacra* parish in 1828, but was included in the civil parish of Kilfinichen and Kilviceon.

Mull is included in the parliamentary constituency of Argyll. The whole island including Tobermory is under the landward administration of Argyll and Bute District Council, within the framework of Strathclyde Region. The offices of the Clerk to the District Council in Mull are in the former police station and sheriff court in Tobermory. In 1979 a new police station was built in the Upper Village. There are three other stations in the island, at Salen, Craignure and Bunessan. Tobermory now has a full-time fire-brigade, with volunteer units at Salen, Craignure and Bunessan.

The whole of Mull is represented in the third-tier body, the Community Council, which takes the place of the former Mull and Iona Council of Social Service. This body has a watching brief and can only make representations to the district council and the region, with no powers to take action. Iona has its own Community Council.

It seems strange that island areas like Mull, Coll and Tiree should be included on the fringes of the huge, unwieldy Region of Strathclyde, whose interests must be predominantly in the industrial South. However, services in Mull appear to have been well maintained since the reorganisation of local government, although at a high cost in revaluation and rating.

EDUCATION

Provisions for local education were only slowly established on Mull, though the island was long influenced, even after the decline of the monastery, by the aura of learning that emanated from Iona.

In the days of the clans the chiefs and leading families sent their children to southern colleges for their schooling; there were no colleges nearer than the southern cities. By the middle of the eighteenth century influential islanders were aware of the need for more education and social polish. A convention of chiefs met at Aros Castle, to consider establishing a centre where Highland youths could receive adequate education. Soon after this the Jacobite uprising of 1745 and the aftermath of Culloden destroyed those local ambitions, and no college was ever established at Aros or anywhere else in Mull during the painful times that followed.

Leading Mull families engaged tutors for their children. For a time Thomas Campbell the poet served in this capacity, at Sunipol, near Calgary, where he learned much of the traditions and folklore of Mull that were to inspire some of his finest works.

However, in addition to the voluntary desire of the chiefs for improvement, there existed a measure of organisation by the central authorities. After the Union of the Crowns in 1603, determined efforts were made by the Privy Council in Edinburgh to set up new standards of culture and education in the Highlands and Islands, but it was only when the Act of 1616 was ratified in 1633, and more organised education was demanded by the powerful Convenanters after 1638, that some improvement took place.

As was the case with other Hebridean islands, the remoteness of Mull discouraged the early establishment of state schools, and it was principally through the efforts of the Church that schools were finally set up. At first a few elementary subjects were taught, but almost entirely to boys. By 1795 there were in Mull three parish schools (one in each parish), one charity school, and four church schools ('for Christian knowledge'). There were a few girls' schools where simple domestic subjects such as spinning and sewing were taught. In the middle of the nineteenth century, these were quaintly described as 'schools of industry for young females'. The fact that one such school was conducted later in the upper storey of Tobermory jail was no reflection at all on the young females: on the contrary, so many years had passed since the jail had been used for its original purpose that some of the unwanted space was turned over for the benefit of the public.

The earliest schools were highly unsuitable. Any hovel could serve and the teachers' emoluments were dishearteningly meagre. The Parochial Schoolmasters' Act of 1803 brought a much needed improvement, and in 1824 a further advance was made when the General Assembly, acting through the local Kirk Sessions, began to finance additional schools. From that time a more effective co-educational system began to develop in Mull.

By 1845 there were seven state schools in Mull. It was unfortunate that at first lessons were taught in the English tongue, in a Gaelic-speaking community. However, this rule was wisely revised soon after, though in any case the English tongue was slowly but surely replacing the native Gaelic. By 1900 there were seventeen schools. In 1986 these had been concentrated into seven: primary schools at Bunessan (29 pupils), Dervaig (28), Iona (9), Lochdonhead (33), Salen (55), Ulva (8); and at Tobermory, both primary (84) and secondary (112) departments. This gives a total of 358 pupils. The total pupil capacity of Mull schools is 532, although accommodation and facilities at Tobermory should be upgraded, and at Salen a new school is being built. For their secondary education, pupils from most of the south of Mull attend Oban High School, with hostel accommodation; those from the rest of Mull attend Tobermory High School. In the 1940s Tobermory was designated a junior secondary school. However, Tobermory is now a four-year secondary school, with a staff of thirteen, presenting candidates for the Scottish

Leaving Certificate 'O' Grade. Officially, it is a senior secondary school.

Pupils from the north of Mull converge on Tobermory for their education by daily conveyances, or are provided with lodgings in the town – not always an easy matter – thus accounting for the seemingly disproportionate pupil numbers in a population of about seven hundred. Accommodated in a school hostel, absent, except at weekends, from the steadying influence of home life, and being taught in classes with less individual attention, achievements in advanced education by pupils from elsewhere in Mull have been less in proportion to those of pupils in the Tobermory area. It is vital for the social structure of the island that rural schools be retained.

Several isolated schools have been closed down through lack of pupils or movements of population, for instance, the tall gaunt building between Ensay and Torloisk which once served the deserted townships of Reudle, Crakaig and the neighbourhood. Scraped into the plaster still remaining on the walls can be seen drawings of old sailing ships left by pupils now long dead.

Adult education has not been neglected. During the winter season classes are held at various centres, ranging from the study of languages, to the making of crooks and sticks, maintenance of chain saws and even first aid for sheep at lambing time!

POOR RELIEF

There were no poor in Mull in the old days when the people were self-supporting. Problems only began to arise when the clan system was destroyed, with its internal care and discipline; they accelerated with an expanding population and an unbalanced economy, and reached dire heights with the collapse of the kelp industry, the Clearances, and the impact of the potato disease.

In 1843, in the parish of Torosay alone, there was an average of twenty-seven cases of abject poverty, each receiving a grant of 12s (60p).

Care of the poor and destitute was a service administered

and financed at first by the Kirk Sessions. Collections for the poor were taken at the churches, and to this were added the fines imposed by the Sessions on people found guilty of immoralities, along with charitable contributions, a service gradually taken over by the parish councils.

After the middle of the nineteenth century Tobermory had become overcrowded with dispossessed and destitute people, desperate for any form of work. Their plight here, and in fact in the whole area in and around Mull, became so bad that the authorities decided to build a central establishment for the care of the poor, not only of the parishes of Mull, but also of Morvern, Arisaig, Ardnamurchan, Coll, Tiree and Moidart. Accordingly, all those parishes co-operated in the building and financing of what was called the Mull Combination Poorhouse, a great rambling building which stood in 5 acres (2ha) of flattish land enclosed by a shining loop of the Tobermory River, just over a mile up the road to Dervaig. It was built in 1862 at a cost of £20,000 on what was originally poor boggy land whose grazing value was only half-a-crown (12½p) per acre, yet these 5 acres (2ha) were feued to the Committee of Management for £24 per annum by the then proprietor of Aros estate. As time went on the land was brought into a condition of productivity, for indeed in the early days there was no lack of workers on the premises.

It was designed to accommodate 140 people in two wings of two storeys, one wing for the men, the other for women. There were fine offices, storerooms, a kitchen, a laundry, bathrooms, a joint dining hall – and even a pulpit for the minister from the Baptist church at Tobermory, who conducted a service at the poorhouse every Sunday afternoon. The buildings were surrounded by walled gardens and fields of oats and potatoes; there were piggeries, a stable, hen-houses, a byre, and a blacksmith's shop, with all necessary tools – everything to preserve the will to work on the part of the unfortunate inmates, who, of course, were at liberty to leave at any time. Their health was taken care of by the doctor from Tobermory, and there was even a well-equipped dispensary for his use in the building.

It was a well-run establishment. People were well cared for, well fed, with a weekly allowance of tobacco for both men and women, with clay pipes provided! However, as time went on, the intensive depopulation of the area, and ultimately the introduction of the Old Age Pensions Act in 1909, caused the numbers to dwindle until by 1924 there were only six inhabitants remaining, all geriatric cases. In the interests of economy they were transferred to Oban and the building was sold to a private buyer for £400. The structure, exploited for copper and lead, was finally allowed to deteriorate into a ruinous eyesore, although under better economic conditions it might have been adapted to other uses. Finally, in the winter of 1973–4, it was completely demolished, except for the lodge, which has been modernised as a private house, together with the inner perimeter wall. The stonework was carried to Tobermory, where it was used to extend the jetty at Ledaig.

THE BURGH OF TOBERMORY

Tobermory is an attractive little town rising in terraces above probably the finest and most picturesque harbour in the Hebrides. It was the smallest burgh in Scotland before reorganisation of local authorities, in 1974, after which, Tobermory was taken over by the Argyll and Bute District Council within the Region of Strathclyde, and since then all services have been administered by these authorities.

The town was created a burgh in 1875. In the petition to the Sheriff of Argyll it is interesting to note the appearance of such names as Yule and Noble, most unusual in Mull. They were the descendants of the East Coast fishing families settled here by the Fisheries Board after Tobermory was established as a fishing station by the British Society for Encouraging Fisheries in 1789 (referred to again later). The impressive courthouse was built in 1862. Here the sheriff held monthly diets until the early 1920s. It now serves as district council offices.

In 1882 an excellent water supply was laid on from a reservoir built 2 miles above the town beside the Dervaig road, at a cost of £6,000. In 1967 it was decided to tap the Mishnish Lochs, a mile further distant, as a main source of supply, and at the same time the old pipes were renewed and choked filters cleared and modernised, at a cost of about £100,000.

In 1966–7 the rateable value of the Burgh was £14,135; that of the whole of Mull was £28,168. In 1986 the rateable value of the whole of Mull was £1,045,312. As the Burgh had been absorbed into the general financial structure of the area, no separate figure for it was available, but it is fair to estimate this in the same proportions as in 1966–7, which would give a figure of approximately £500,000.

In 1970 the Burgh owned sixty-two houses. By 1986 this

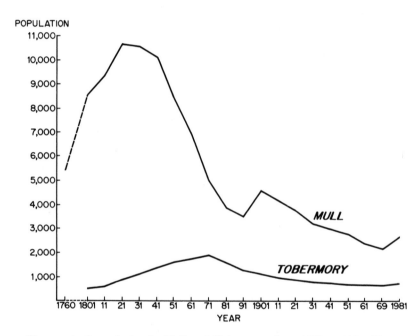

The trend of population in Mull and Tobermory from 1760 to 1981. The rapid growth of the eighteenth century reached a peak in 1821, after the return of soldiers from the Napoleonic wars. While the island's population fell steadily thereafter, the number of people in Tobermory itself rose to a maximum about 1871 as the evictions gradually cleared many of the country settlements. Since 1969 there has been some increase in Mull's population, though that in Tobermory has remained about level, perhaps reflecting the growing elderly population seeking peaceful retirement years figure had increased to seventy-eight under the Argyll and Bute District Council. Housing and public services have been maintained at a high standard under the new administration.

In 1969, to mark the fiftieth anniversary of the setting-up of the Forestry Commission, the policies of the former Aros House on the South side of the Bay were handed over by the commission to the burgh as a public park. About the turn of the century the Allan family gifted to the people of Tobermory the two-storey building known as the Aros Hall, containing a library, reading and committee rooms and a billards room. The hall itself could seat three hundred. The building is now run by the district council.

Tobermory's chief economic disadvantage – especially now that the harbour focus has moved to Craignure – is its lack of small industries. The remoteness from mainland markets, and high freight costs inhibit the establishing of other than high-value types of industry.

The population of Tobermory has, like that of the whole island, fluctuated widely over the last 250 years. There were fewer than 200 folk there when it was established as a fishing port in 1789. The maximum population for Mull was recorded in 1821, while in Tobermory, with rural depopulation, the maximum was reached fifty years later.

Year	Population of whole island	Population of Tobermory[*]
1789	—	200
1801	8,539	456
1811	9,383	550
1821	10,612	850
1851	8,369	1,540
1871	5,017	1,850
1891	3,465	1,265
1911	4,173	900
1921	3,754	850
1931	3,160	772
1951	2,693	693
1961	2,343	668
1969	2,100	610
1981	2,365	683[**]

  * For years when census figures have been unobtainable, estimates based on official reports and other sources have been used.

  ** For the first time figures represent actual permanent residents.

By the middle of the nineteenth century the number of people in Tobermory had soared with the influx of dispossessed families seeking locally in Tobermory what Mull people now emigrate to seek in the industrial South – security of employment. A witness before the Land Court at the end of the last century had this to say of the town:

> There is not a poorer place than Tobermory; for when the people were swept away from their lands and houses they had to take refuge in barns and behind dykes; and all kinds of outhouses were brought into requisition to shelter the people driven away from their places.

In 1892, in spite of the benefits of Poor Relief, there were seventeen families in Tobermory bordering on abject poverty. Like the rest of Mull, Tobermory was to see its population dwindle away through lack of work and through the attractions of the mainland.

Page 139: (above) Iona Cathedral – looking across the Sound of Iona to Mull, with Eilean nam Ban, Women's Island, in left middle distance; (below) Crakaig, Treshnish, a deserted village (Scottish Tourist Board)

Page 140: (top) A fine Cellini cannon recovered from the Armada ship sunk in Tobermory Bay, now standing in front of Inveraray Castle, home of the Duke of Argyll in whom rights of recovery of items found in the wreck are vested; *(centre)* The SS *Grenadier* at Tobermory Pier about 1926. A salvage ship operating on the site of the Sunken Armada ship is in the background; *(below)* Opening day of the Mull and West Highland Narrow Gauge Railway Company Limited at the Craignure terminus

9   *THE ISLAND CULTURE*

The mysticism of the ancient Celts, the quick change from depression to gaiety, the vivid imagination, are still found in Mull. The islanders' character was forged in fighting for survival against other clans, against disease, poverty and famine, even against the elements, and, seemingly, in the worst struggle of all, during the eighteenth and nineteenth centuries, against the despairing thought that both God and man were heedless of their existence.

As workers the Mull folk are slow, methodical and conscientious, but only a prejudiced or ignorant stranger would dare to describe them as lazy and shiftless, an insult that may arise from the curious belief that the industrial South has a monopoly of efficiency and hard work. Emigrants from Mull, a supposedly unprogressive environment, have participated in the pioneer movements that established the first outposts of the former British Empire.

Nowadays the younger generation conforms much to the fashions and habits of its mainland counterpart, thanks to the brainwashing, if you like, of broadcasting, and to the telephone and better communications. The kilt is no longer worn as a regular article of dress except by a rare enthusiast, who is usually a visitor! Still, under the thin veneer of sophistication, the islanders retain a 'clannishness' and a character all of their own.

Mull people who live and work far from the island tend to congregate in order to preserve the atmosphere of home. In 1866 the Mull and Iona Association was formed in Glasgow with the objects of providing opportunities to meet, to foster the art, literature and music of Mull, and to assist cases of distress among their people. It has been an active association ever since and the annual concert – the 'Mull and Iona' – still follows the old traditions.

141

THE ISLAND CULTURE

The progressive unification of the British Isles has involved the gradual suppression of regional social characteristics; in the case of Gaelic speech, as of Welsh, it has survived longest, in the remoter western enclaves and islands. In Mull, there has been a change from the monoglot use of Gaelic, through a stage during the nineteenth century of the English tongue being generally understood, to a present-day situation in which Gaelic is spoken only by the older generation. In 1881, 88 per cent of the population could speak Gaelic; in 1981, only about 25 per cent. In 1881 there were 800 people who could speak only Gaelic; in 1981 there were none. The Burgh of Tobermory, as one might expect, has always shown a lower proportion of Gaelic speakers – about 4 per cent below the average figure for Mull – through the presence of a large proportion of residents not indigenous to the island and its traditonal ways.

Census year	Speaking both Gaelic and English	Speaking Gaelic only	Speaking English only	Total population
1881	3,395*	800+*	431	3,826
1891	2,351	634	480	3,465
1901	3,293	454	810	4,557
1911	3,056	209	908	4,173
1921	2,595	83	1,076	3,754
1931	2,254	35	871	3,160
1951	1,281	15	1,397	2,693
1961	882	2	1,459	2,343
1981	628	—	1,937	2,565**

* For 1881, the figure for those speaking Gaelic only is included in the figure in the first column (ie the first column includes all Gaelic speakers, whether or not they spoke English as well).

** In the 1981 census the people actually resident on that date numbered 2,921, including visitors. The correct figure for population normally resident was 2,565.

Deterioration in the state of the Gaelic language accelerated since 1872 when a national statutory system of education was established in Scotland, in which the English language was

142

the medium of instruction. Education has long been valued by the islanders, but in the question of the language, the desire to learn has conflicted with their cultural heritage. Until about seventy years ago it was considered a social offence to be heard talking in Gaelic within the precincts of certain schools – a situation that left some of the children almost tongue-tied. The paucity of modern literature, even of school-books, published in Gaelic, and the evolution of the English language itself in a time of technological change have added to the difficulties of survival for the Gaelic language.

From the domestic angle, it is said that if the mother is the Gaelic speaker, a child has ten times more chance of picking up Gaelic than a child whose father is the only Gaelic-speaker – veritably a mother-tongue.

Gaelic has been described as plastic, copious and expressive. This is brought out in a picturesque manner by the writer Fionn MacColla in *The Albanach*, where he says: 'Now in our own Gaelic a man can't tell his name itself without every man will know his whole history and his people's before him; and the name of every place will be a picture of what will be there, so that a man will almost know a place on first seeing it by its likeness to the name that will be on it.' The finer shades of Gaelic meaning cannot be adequately translated into English, a feature best summarised by the man involved in a heated discussion who averred in exasperation: 'I would tell you what I thought of you in the Gaelic, if I thought you had the education!' The spoken English of the islands is soft, slow and lilting, and in the voices of children fascinating to hear. It is grammatically pure, subject only to lapses in construction caused by speaking a form of English which is basically translated Gaelic, as for example, 'I will be going' instead of 'I am going.'

While every area of the British Isles has its own dialect, and the Mull folk are no exception, they are critical of what they regard as the exaggerated, rather slurred 'English' accent heard over the air in broadcasting, on stage and elsewhere which poses as standard English. To the Mull ear, the letter 'r' is – in 'standard' English – slurred, omitted or intrusive. The voice over the air seems not to distinguish between 'h' and 'wh', while diphthongs take the place of straight vowels, in, for example, the 'o', 'oo' and 'a' sounds. For instance, 'more' and 'moor' sound exactly the same. Mull natives hear the voice speak of the 'Shore of Pezzia' instead of the Shah of Persia. A wheel-chair becomes 'weel chay'; score-board becomes 'sco-bode'. 'Wat', 'wen' and 'wear' are self-evident, as is 'give it a will' for 'give it a whirl'. Southerners in turn point out that the islanders (and Scots as a whole) exaggerate the 'r' and 'wh' sounds and the sibilants.

PLACE NAME ELEMENTS

The descriptive and imaginative nature of the Gaelic tongue is revealed in topographical names in Mull. Some place names perpetuate the personal names of people – real or mythical – who once lived on the island, the actual memory of whose deeds or fame has long since been lost. Examples of this kind are: Loch Sguabain, Sgeir Charistiona, Kilninian, Kilbrennan and Kilpatrick.

Other place names are either entirely Norse in origin, especially on the western side of the island and round the coasts, or have Norse elements in them, for example Rossal, Scridain, Burg, Fors, Loch Frisa and Nish. Norse names persisted in hunting, grazing, woodlands, and of course in coastal configurations forming sailing marks. This is revealed in the proportions of Norse to Gaelic names relating to the decreasing density of Norse settlements from the northern to the southern Hebrides. According to *Norsk Geografisk Tiddescrift*, Vol 22, No 1 (1968), here are the proportions:

	Norse	Gaelic
Lewis	4	1
Skye	3	2
Mull	2	2
Islay	1	2
Kintyre	1	4
Arran	1	8

Some place names are known only by an Anglicised version of their original form, such as: Ballygown (*baile*, homestead, and *gobhainn*, blacksmith); Ben (*beann*, a mountain); Knock (*cnoc*, a ridge).

A few names have no exact English equivalent. The original word form has been lost, through gradual changes in local dialects which have taken place over the long period of time when such records were by the spoken, and not the written, word; the only clue to its original meaning is given in the hearsay provided by the older people. Word forms like the 'Mish' of Mishnish, or Urgabul are examples.

STORY-TELLING

It may seem strange that superstition should have figured so strongly in the lives of a religious people like the inhabitants of Mull, whose religion seems to have been kept isolated from the beliefs and practices of the distant pagan background.

The early island-dwellers lived very close to nature, and explained away any unaccountable happenings as the work of supernatural beings, fairies, or the 'little folks' (both benevolent and malevolent), giants, water-horses, witches, an unseen horde, until education and modern sophistication submerged the old way of life.

In the great days of clan culture the seannachies, or wise men, the successors to the Druid priests, were the recorders, counsellors and geneaologists of the chiefs. But while word-perfect in this type of memory work, they were doubtless only human in the correct memorising of more intricate subjects over a long period, when there were no written records. Ritual and ceremonial, as well as romantic stories, might come to differ considerably from the original. The seannachies are gone long ago, but something of their art has come down in story-telling; and indeed Mull is outstanding among the Hebridean islands for both its gifted raconteurs and the volume of its tales. Many of these stories are now being collected and preserved in the printed word, otherwise they will be lost for ever with the passing of this generation of old story-tellers who alone preserve the knowledge.

Stories may concern three types of subject; traditions and folklore, witchcraft and superstitious, and second sight and

145

the supernatural. While witchcraft is a premeditated art, sponsored by the Evil One (according to a sixteenth century Act of the Scottish Parliament), second sight is quite involuntary and can be an embarrassment to the possessor.

Among the Gaelic-speaking people of Mull humour in story-telling is natural, spontaneous, and closer to the things of daily life, usually with the 'punch' in the last line. The art of exaggeration is freely drawn upon. This is brought out by two examples. The first is attributed to Callum nan Croig, reputed to have been Mull's greatest raconteur, who lived around the end of the nineteenth century.

> I wass good at tying the flies, for fishing, you know. One night I wass busy at the kitchen table getting some ready to go to the loch next morning. Well, ass fast ass I wass finishing one, I would put it down on the table to get on with the next, but when I looked up again it wass gone! The next one I tied I chust put it down, sat back and lit my pipe and watched. Do you know, I wass tying them that good the spiders wass coming down from the roof to take them away.

The art of repartee is also well developed. Never be deceived by the deceptive slowness of a Mull man. One day the Staffa and Iona cruise boat was tied up beside Tobermory pier with a full complement of passengers. One of them leaning over the rail nudged his companions and, indicating a shabby uncouth figure standing seemingly vacantly at the edge of the pier, he remarked, 'Watch me take a rise out of that chap.' Pointing to the tall Marconi wireless pole (the 'Big Pole') which stood for many years above the village, the tourist called out, 'I say, my man, can you tell me what fruit grows on that tree?' Back came the immediate answer, 'Inteet yess, sir; electric currants'.

MUSIC

Mull folk have music in their blood. In the words of an old song: 'Morvern for sword play, Mull for a song.' Music was another legacy brought to Mull by the monks of Iona. St Columba was himself a musician who had been taught in

Ireland. The traditional instruments were the harp (*clarsach*) and the timpan, a six- or eight-stringed instrument played with a bow or plectrum. Although much traditional music and art was destroyed in the successive sackings of Iona by the Norsemen, much survived, and after the end of the Norse invasion the clan system developed, and for the next three to four hundred years Celtic art and music developed and flourished. Every chief had his harper and poet, virtually a court herald. The warlike times of the Middle Ages led to the decline of the harp and the adoption of the bagpipes as a stimulating influence for fighting clans. This was a very ancient instrument: one early Greek coin bears the impression of a man playing an instrument closely resembling the Highland bagpipes. At first the bagpipes were simpler, with two drones instead of the three adopted later. At the beginning of the seventeenth century there was a pipers' college in Ulva run by the McArthurs, hereditary pipers to the MacDonalds and second only to the MacCrimmons, of Skye, with whom McArthur had received his training. The Rankins were pipers to the Macleans of Duart. The great piper Morrison, of Ardtun, Bunessan, even set up a school of piping in New South Wales!

In *The Lost Pibroch* Neil Munro says: 'To the make of a piper go seven years of his own learning and seven generations before. If it is in it will out . . . if not, let him take to the net or the sword.' Let the critic of the bagpipes put aside prejudice and prejudgment and substitute a measure of toleration and concentration, but, above all, hear the pipes played by a first-class exponent in the natural setting – in woodlands, or across water. Then all of a sudden he may 'stand at the start of knowledge, and leaning a fond ear to the drones he may have parley with old folks of old affairs . . . stand by the cairn of Kings, ken the colour of Fingal's hair, and see the moon-glint on the hook of the Druids!'

Probably the social evolution of the people is expressed more vividly in music than in the written word. At the national Mod, the annual festival of Gaelic music and language organised by An Comunn Gaidhealach (The Gaelic Society), natives of the island have repeatedly been awarded the gold medal, the top award, not only as individuals, but also as families, for example the MacMillan sisiters of Dervaig whose voices first enthralled audiences in the 1930s. Mary MacDonald, a simple country woman born in 1817 in the Ross of Mull with no knowledge of written or spoken English, composed that lovely hymn that is translated as 'Child in the Manger'. Greatest of all the songs of Mull is the anthem of the island, *An t'Eilean Muileach* (The Isle of Mull), a song from the heart by Dugald MacPhail (1818–87) the bard from Strath Coil, written and composed when working in distant Newcastle.

Naturally, the music of Mull has the sea in it, most forcibly interpreted in the *iorram* or rowing songs, in which the rowers, swinging in unison, used to sing in a kind of undertone one of these exquisitely beautiful songs, half recitative, half melody, with a rousing chorus in which all the occupants of the boat joined, in time with the swing of the oars, the click of the thole pins and the quick slap of wavelets against the bow. There are also gay and rollicking airs with mischievous wit, such as *Callum Bheag* (Wee Callum) a song of forty-six verses describing the highly imaginative voyage to Glasgow and back by a man who had never before been in a boat! Music was the medium which used to lighten manual work such as weaving, milking, butter-making and waulking (shrinking the newly woven cloth). Love songs have a wistfulness and sadness all of their own, while the dance music gay and enegetic, overlaps into another style of singing, the *Port-a'Beul*, or mouth music. This is a rapid, rhythmical, tongue-twisting, repetitive style of singing, imitative of the bagpipes and often used when the services of a piper were not available. Wherever a Mull man finds himself he is transported back to the island in imagination by a few bars of one of its nostalgic songs – 'Mull of the High Cool Hills', 'Mull of the Mountains', 'Fionnphort Ferry', 'The Sound of Mull', 'The Boatman'. 'Leaving Lismore'; scores of songs, some going back for centuries, such as 'The Sound of Mull', adapted as a sad love song from a chant attributed to the Iona monks. In the words of Yeats:

I hear lake water lapping with low sounds on the shore;
While I stand on the roadway, or on the pavement gray,
I hear it in the deep heart's core.

A popular instrument today is the violin. At Glengorm in 1910 there was a fiddle band eight strong! Choral singing was becoming more and more popular, and Mull set up its own four-part choirs after World War I, although they faded out after a few years.

Nowadays the popularity of the piano-accordion fully equals that of the violin, with the guitar in the background. After World War II Mull saw the appearance of famous international exponents of the piano-accordion like Bobby MacLeod and Callum MacLean, who not only kept the love of music alive in Mull, but aroused public interest, to such an extent that, in 1977, along with a dedicated group of enthusiasts, they inaugurated the Mull Musical Festival Society, which has proved so successful that in the last week of April annually the festival takes over the island and attracts the country's most famous exponents of our national music on traditional instruments.

DRAMA AND ART

Within the local communities life has tended to become narrower. There are still ceilidhs and concerts, and the activities of church organisations, the Women's Rural Institute, drama groups, and so on. The schools have taken up drama activities with enthusiasm, and the children have distinguished themselves in open competitions. However, since the coming of radio and television people tend to keep more to their own firesides and there is not quite as much public involvement as in the past.

A new theatre development was inaugurated in 1965 when the Mull Little Theatre opened at Dervaig. Mentioned as the smallest professional theatre in the world in the *Guinness Book of Records*, it could seat an audience of no more than forty. Its summer programme of serious modern plays was widely acclaimed throughout the country, for the little company went on tour away from its native Mull. The principals were two enterprising people, Barry and Marianne Hesketh, who were both experienced in broadcasting and stagecraft. All the parts were acted or spoken by the two principals, sometimes with the aid of puppets and tape recordings. In recognition of their work the two principals were awarded the OBE. The company has been reorganised as a private limited company, the Dervaig Arts Theatre Ltd. Sadly, Marianne died in 1984.

In the superb setting of Carsaig Bay, in the south of Mull – and surely there can be no more spectacular or appropriate a situation – a residential school of painting was opened in 1967 by Julia Wroughton, ARCA, ARWA, at her home, Inniemore Lodge, where between April and October about two hundred amateur artists are catered for.

Then in the mid-1970s the Old Byre Heritage Centre opened near Dervaig in a roomy two-storey outbuilding. Originally a museum of early farming and domestic equipment, it developed into a heritage centre giving a vivid picture of nineteenth-century Mull in a tableau of audio-dramatisation. On the top floor two typical rooms of the time were shown, one of a simple cottar, the other of a more well-to-do farmer – who would have been known as a tacksman. The audio programme, recorded by knowledgeable local people, described the old way of life, the daily pursuits, and dark memories of the Clearances. The ground floor was given over to a tea-room and display of crafts. It was deservedly the winner of the two national awards for its dramatic representation of crofting life.

Mull, its background and topography, have attracted film directors; in fact, no less than four major films have been on location here: *I know Where I'm Going*, *Madam Sin*, *Where Eight Bells Toll*, and *The Eye of the Needle*.

OUTDOOR ACTIVITIES

In summer, when time allowed, the menfolk used to compete in strenuous athletics, trials of strength such as weight-lifting, putting the stone, or tossing the caber. This last sport, now formalised at Highland games throughout the country, (Tobermory has its annual Highland Games) is said to have originated from the skill and strength needed to raise the cabers or rafters when building the roofs of houses. Wrestling and running were popular. According to *The Gael*, men of past generations are visualised as: 'leaping from crag to crag and engaging in manly sports demanding brawn and muscle, or crossing dirks and claymores at the tiniest hint of a personal insult'. Dr Johnson and Boswell had as their guide in Mull Col Maclean (Maclean of Coll), who could 'run down a greyhound, adjusting his pace, which the dog would not'.

Formerly the young men of Mull were keen on the game of shinty, a free-style form of hockey, and exciting matches used to be held on New Year's Day and other rare holidays up to the turn of the nineteenth century. It is played very little now in the island.

Since 1980 an enthusiastic rugby club has been in existence, with a surprisingly high standard of play, considering the small population of the island. A suitable permanent playing field has still to be acquired.

Also in July there is held the popular Clyde to Tobermory yacht race; in August there is the Tobermory Regatta, and the log-established Salen Agricultural Show. Clay-pigeon shoots, sheep-dog trials and ploughing matches – using the modern tractor instead of horses – are held regularly, and in early October the major and highly spectacular Motor Car Rally is held by the 2300 Car Club of Blackburn. Such events bring large numbers of visitors to the island.

Yachting has its local followers (there is an enthusiastic yachting club at Tobermory) and the attractions of the seas and lochs around Mull bring thousands of yachtsmen from all over Britain, with Tobermory as the centre. Increasing numbers of young people are coming to explore Mull, and a hostel, open all summer, has been set up in Tobermory by the Scottish Youth Hostels Association.

Early in the 1900s there was a wave of interest in golf in Mull. Courses were laid out at Calgary, Glengorm, Salen and Craignure, in addition to the older sporting little course in Tobermory, as well as one in Iona. Facilities were somewhat primitive, and the courses were all of nine holes or fewer; however, enthusiasm was high, and for a few years inter-club

151

matches were played. The Tobermory course, overlooking the harbour and the Sound of Mull, has one of the most picturesque situations in the Hebrides. Established in 1896, it was moved for many yeas to the fields opposite the poorhouse, a mile up the road to Dervaig. It returned to its original home of Erray (above the north of Tobermory) in the 1930s. It is a nine-hole course of 2,324yd (2,125m), with a standard scratch score of 64, and its many hazards make good scoring anything but easy. It is now run by the Western Isles Hotel, whose guests are entitled to free use of the course, and it is open to visitors.

The little course in Iona is still in active use, and in 1979 the nine-hole course at Craignure was reopened. In time it is hoped to extend this to eighteen holes. The other little courses disappeared long ago.

Angling enthusiasts will find plenty of scope in Mull, for every loch and burn has its indigenous stock of brown trout. Salmon and sea-trout fishing is limited by the terrain, but some is easily obtained on private waters on payment of reasonable fees. In Loch Torr, for instance (an artificial loch made about 1900), a Tobermory syndicate offers visitors brown trout, sea-trout, rainbow-trout and salmon, and has two boats on the loch.

Tobermory Angling Club now issues permits for fishing on the Aros Lake (which has brown and rainbow-trout, including some of large size which escaped from the fish enclosures and became established) and on the Mishnish Lochs (brown trout only, up to 2–3lb (900g–1.3kg)) which are regularly restocked and on which three boats are available. The Tackle Shop, Tobermory, issues permits for fishing Loch Torr and Loch Sguabain, as well as for a number of Mull's best salmon rivers. There are Loch Frisa, Loch and River Ba (expensive), Loch Assapol, and Loch Poit-I near Bunessan, so there is no lack of fishing waters.

However, it is in sea-angling that Mull excels; in fact, round its coasts is found the best sea-fishing in Europe. Fishing from Tobermory boats with rod and line, eight Scottish and British record fish have been landed, and no less than twenty-eight different species of fish have been caught within a single week.

Tobermory is the most popular centre, and boats from the Tackle Shop are booked a year ahead by enthusiastic anglers; and not without reason, for during one season, that of 1984, 400 fish included in the total catches each weighed over 100lb (45kg) – all taken on rod and line. The largest, a common skate, weighed 202lb (91.5kg).

FAMOUS MULL PEOPLE

Up to the seventeenth and eighteenth centuries, Mull was famous for its doctors, who were referred to simply as the *Ollamhan Muileach*, or Mull doctors. They were members of the Beaton family who lived at Pennyghael, where the enclosure in which medical herbs were grown used to be pointed out by the older residents. They were hereditary physicians to the Lords of the Isles and later to the Macleans of Duart. They appear to have come from Béthune in the Pas-de-Calais about the twelfth century.

The Beatons traditionally passed on their medical skill from father to son. Medical manuscripts which are still preserved (in the Advocates' Library, Edinburgh, in the British Museum and in a few private collections) not only record the ancient arts of medicine, but also the genealogy of the family. There are still Beatons in Mull, but no direct link with the famous doctors can now be traced.

There is a story told about John Beaton, who was said to be the greatest doctor of his time, whose simple advice to the people in his care was 'to be cheerful, temperate and early risers'. He was summoned to appear before the King of Scotland, probably James VI, in Edinburgh along with twenty-four other leading physicians, to undergo a test which would decide who was the most skilled among them.

The king feigned an illness, and the test for each medical man was to diagnose it without seeing the royal patient. A specimen of urine was provided for examination, which, however, was not that of the King. Beaton was the only one to call his bluff, and for his discernment he was admitted to royal favour. In fact, it is recorded that in 1609 James VI granted a charter to Fergus McBeath, of Ballinaby, possibly the son of the same Dr John, conferring on him the office of Chief Physician of the Isles as well as his hereditary title to lands, favours which presumably were connected with Dr John's successful consultation in Edinburgh.

Shortly after his success – perhaps even on his way home – poison was administered to him secretly by his jealous rivals, who with a healthy respect for his skill first of all took the precaution of hiding all the antidotes for which the expiring doctor called in his last agonies.

The medical branch died out in Mull in the early eighteenth century. Rev Dugald Campbell, writing in the *Statistical Report* of 1795, mentions a 'large folio MS in Gaelic, treating of physic, which was left with a woman, the heiress of the Beatons, seen by some now living; but what became of it the incumbent [Campbell], after all his enquiries, could not find. It is perhaps lost, as the heirs of this woman are quite illiterate.' Thus ended a family tradition of medical science traceable back to the learned monks of Iona.

The memory of the Beatons is preserved in a cairn erected above the shore of Loch Scridain near Pennyghael. It is surmounted by a plain cross whose shaft bore the initials of two of the Beaton family and the date: G M B   1582   D M B. The lettering can now hardly be traced.

The great missionary and explorer Dr David Livingstone, of Blantyre, had close family connections with Mull, for his grandfather was a crofter from the island of Ulva. There is a romantic historical background to this. The Livingstone family, whose lineage went back for four hundred years, were living at Ballachulish, in north Argyll at the time of that despicable miscarriage of justice in 1752 when James Stewart, James of the Glen, was strongly arrested and convicted at Inveraray for the murder of Campbell of Glenure.

The body of James of the Glen was hung in chains under military guard from a gibbet above the present bridge at Ballachulish, not far from the scene of the murder. It remained for three years and when the bones fell apart they were wired together. Three of the Livingstone brothers conspired to remove the remains and destroy the gibbet; one was to entice the soldier on guard along to the inn for a drink, the other two were to do the deed. The plan was successful, but fearing the consequences the two chief conspirators left the district, crossed over to Mull, and settled in Ulva as crofters. One of them, Niall Mor (Big Neil) left Ulva after a dispute with the factor, went to Glasgow and then settled in Blantyre. His son, Niall Bheag (Little Neil) was the father of Dr David Livingstone.

A colourful sixteenth-century islander was Ailean nan Sop (Allan of the Straw), so called because his first act on being born on a pallet of straw in the kitchen was to grasp a handful of straw. He was brother of Eachann Mor, twelfth chief of Duart. As a youth he took to the sea and, throwing in his lot with the Danes, who still sometimes raided the islands, he rose to be admiral of their raiding fleet and the fiercest pirate that ever roamed the Hebrides. Later he gave up his roving life and retired to his native Loch Tuath (after killing his wicked stepfather who had wronged him in early life) where he is (incorrectly) said to have founded the family of the Macleans of Torloisk. His tomb is in Iona, where his body lies under the slabs of Relig Oran.

One of the most famous members of the Clan Maclean was Sir Fitzroy Donald Maclean, chief of the clan and twenty-fifth of his line, who after a lapse of ownership for 220 years purchased back the ancestral home, Duart Castle, which was restored and formally opened in 1912. Sir Fitzroy, who had fought in the Crimean War, died in 1936 after reaching his 101st year. The present chief, formerly Sir Charles H. F. Maclean, now Lord Maclean, was raised to the peerage in 1971 and was Lord Chamberlain to the Royal Household. He is Lord Lieutenant of Argyll and was formerly Chief Scout, and during his extensive travelling in that office he carried the name of Mull into almost every corner of the world.

The late Neil Cameron, who belonged to Tobermory, rose to be head of a large fashion and textile business in Sunderland. He it was who donated £50,000 to expedite the building of Craignure Pier.

Prominent public figures have come to live in Mull, including the late Lord Butler and the well-known actor Paul Scofield, with houses between Dervaig and Calgary.

The island has sent many high-ranking officers to every war of the last 250 years – which recalls the cynical words of William Pitt at the time of the Napoleonic Wars: 'I have found a new use for Highlanders: they make good cannon fodder.' In the Napoleonic Wars up to 1815 there served in the British Army five generals, one lieutenant-general, three major-generals, seventeen colonels, three lieutenant-colonels, eight majors and seventy-eight officers of lower rank. During the same period one admiral and a number of officers served in the Navy, mainly in the Marines. Many of those men were Macleans, and the rank and file of Mull men would themselves have made a formidable army, many of the tenants following the laird to the wars. Conditions were different when it came to the Crimean War and the Indian Mutiny. Only a handful of men served at the Crimea, including the then Col Sir Fitzroy Maclean. The people of Mull could well have repeated the words uttered by an old Ross-shire man during a recruiting rally at the time of the Crimean War. When Lord Stafford, who had married the Duchess of Sutherland (whose lands had been subjected to the most oppressive clearances) expressed his disappointment that so few tenants had volunteered to join the army, and old man cried: 'The people are all gone; you can send your sheep!'

The father of Maj-Gen Lachlan MacQuarie, Governor General of New South Wales from 1810–21, was a farmer in Ulva, and his mother lived latterly at Oskamull Farm. Maj Gen MacQuarie earned the name of Father of Australia on account of his successful administrative ability, and only jealousy on the part of certain members of the government at home prevented him from the bestowal of greater honours. He bought the Mull estate of Jarvisfield (now Gruline, at the end of Loch Ba) and established the village of Salen in 1800. His body lies, with those of members of his family, in the private mausoleum at Gruline. The old Volunteers of the last century, and the later Territorials, attracted numbers of Mull men. Like so many of the islands, Mull sent a higher than average proportion to the two world wars, especially into the Navy and merchant navy. The Argyll and Sutherland Highlanders was naturally the regiment most favoured, together with the

Page 160: (above) Kelp burning on Inch Kenneth c1800; *(below)* Weighing and boxing salmon for the Glasgow fish market

Page 159: (*above*) A young descendant of the old black Highland kyloe;
(*below left*) Home-carved crooks exhibited at the Salen Show;
(*below right*) A very old leister (salmon spear) made by an island blacksmith,
found in the bed of a Mull river

Page 158: (above) Achafraoch House – Mull Combination Poorhouse – c1920 when still occupied; (below) The quiet little village of Dervaig, north-west Mull, described as 'the most picturesque in the Hebrides'

Page 157: (*above*) Tobermory: the main street and the old and new piers; (*below*) Tobermory c1800. All the buildings, except the high-roofed one on extreme left, are still standing. The building opposite the pier entrance was the Mull Hotel; of that next to it is now the Post Office (*Collection of A.D. Brown*)

Argyll Mountain Battery and the Scottish Horse.

Typical of the inshore crofter-fishermen of Mull were the MacDougall family, who fished entirely for their own requirements until the export of lobsters became profitable. There were two families, who lived at Haunn, Treshnish, where their buildings existed from the beginning of the nineteenth century and may still be seen, some in ruins, some converted to holiday cottages.

One of the last surviving members of the families was Alick MacDougall, known as Alick Ban (fair); he was also known as the Rubber Man because of his great strength and endurance, in spite of having a leg crippled by an accident when serving in the Royal Navy during World War I. Well loved in the community, he spoke Gaelic in preference to English and had a store of old Gaelic songs, most of which regrettably died with him unrecorded in 1961. He also had a wide knowledge of local lore and history, for he had spent his whole life on and beside the seas and islands around Mull. Alick's words on first going out of doors in the morning were never, 'What's the weather like?' but 'How's the tide?'

One of his stories reflects the experience and supreme confidence of the hardy fishermen in handling a boat. One morning during World War II, he rose early to prepare his gear for setting lobster creels. In his latter years he was no longer living at Haunn, but at Quinish, 2 miles north of Dervaig, where his tiny cottage and store stood beside a natural jetty formed by a geological dyke in the sheltered inlet. Then (in his own words):

As I was going to the jetty I saw this big mine, with its horns sticking up, floating in with the tide not fifty yards from the shore. I knew that if this went off it would blow the boat and the house, and maybe myself, to bits. So I got a length of pig-iron from what I used as ballast, lashed a rope to it, and put it in the stern of my dinghy I kept tied up to the jetty. I pushed her off with the oars and backed up to the mine. Well, I got a grip on it by the bottom of two of the horns and turned it over 'till I came to a ring bolt; so I tied the end of the rope to that and pushed the mine away, then dropped the pig-iron over the side for an anchor. I rowed to the shore, had my breakfast, then walked into Dervaig to get them to telephone the Mine Disposal. Man, I wouldn't care for their job! When they were making the mine safe I was half a mile up the hill behind a rock with my hands over my ears.

Donald Morrison (1885–1986), one of the last of the old generation of gifted oral and musical traditionalists, died in 1986 aged 101. He was born on a croft at Ardtun, in the Ross of Mull, where for five generations his family had been tenants of the Duke of Argyll. Between 1953 and 1976 he provided the School of Scottish Studies with many recordings, mostly in Gaelic, as well as old songs by forgotten Mull bards which would otherwise have been lost for ever.

FUNERALS

Up to the earliest years of the twentieth century funerals, were not always decorous. Extravagant sums of money were raised even by the poorest families in order to provide a funeral with all the traditional hospitality, even to parting with their last horse or cow. This generally included a quota of spirits; when this became too generous trouble sometimes started. In fact, back in the days when illicit distilling was prevalent the generosity of the family was measured by the number of kegs provided.

Long distances had often to be covered by the cortège, the coffin being carried on wooden bearers by relays of mourners, or on a horse-drawn cart. Every wayfarer on the road was invited to accept a drink 'to the health of the corpse', and to refuse was something of an insult. Old people will still tell you tales of days when the mourners arrived at the place of interment with so much drink taken that they found they had left the coffin behind at some halting-place back along the road, or it had even fallen unnoticed off the open back of the cart on some extra-steep hill.

Along a number of Mull roads there are little cairns of stones at the summits of steep hills, or beside water. Some of these mark where the cortèges halted for a rest. On departing, every mourner left a stone until a little cairn was built up. This may have connections with a very early custom of placing small stones or pebbles beside the bodies of the dead, as was found in the crypt of Iona Cathedral.

At remote cemeteries relatives sometimes had to dig the grave themselves. A macabre story concerns a young man industriously digging in the old family grave. Presently he stooped down and picked up a skull he had just uncovered, and held it up for inspection. 'This will be my grandfather', he announced proudly; 'Man, man, had he no' a grand set of teeth!'

It may surprise readers that the resurrection-men, or body-snatchers, operated in Mull, certainly up to the 1880s. It was quite common for local men and relatives of the deceased to take it in turn to watch over a new grave for the fortnight or so after the interment. The writer's father remembered, as a boy in about 1870, seeing the watchers sitting against a wall of Pennygown cemetery under a sheltering tarpaulin, with a loaded gun beside them and a cheerful fire of driftwood for company. In the old cemetery at Tobermory a tombstone, now damaged and recumbent, lying near the upper boundary wall, has a hole through the centre made by a bullet fired one night at grave-robbers.

This trade (if it be so called) existed between the island and the anatomists of the Glasgow medical college. The retail price paid by the agent to local operators for a reasonably fresh corpse was £5. The local agent was a man not unfamiliar with the medical profession, who was unmarried and lived all by himself on the outskirts of the town. He prepared the goods for transhipment in casks of brine, which were shipped as normal cargo direct from Tobermory to Glasgow.

Although suspected of the practice, the agent was never identified until one night a fearsome prank was played on him by a party of young sparks from the town, just after an interment had taken place in the local cemetery. The negro cook from a visiting ship entered into the spirit of the operation and allowed himself to be tied up in a large sack, which was delivered after dark at the back door of the unsuspecting doctor. He handed out the usual £5 note to the dim figures, and dragged the sack into the kitchen. When he bent down by the light of a candle to begin his preparations, the sack slit open from within, and a fist emerged holding a gleaming knife, followed by a grinning black face. The sheer horror expressed by the doctor as he fled from the premises was enjoyed by the watching conspirators, who had not only proved their case, but had a £5 note to share between them.

10 *FARMS AND FORESTS*

From the earliest times people were attracted to Mull by its fertile soil, which gave an adequate return even with primitive methods of cultivation. The system that evolved and continued to the 19th century for the working of arable land was the lazy-bed, strips of land allocated by a locally elected committee on a rotational basis, which meant that there was no incentive to improve the soil beyond the expected period of tenure. Shell sand was used as a substitute for lime, with seaweed, manure accumulated during the wintering of stock, even soot impregnated thatch when it was replaced on houses. Crop yields were low. Potatoes, introduced in the middle of the 18th century, became the most important crop. The caschrom, or foot plough, was a cumbersome but effective forerunner of the spade, for it was most useful in turning over the soil and turf in small patches among rocks.

Methods of drainage improved; drainage was an important factor, allowing hitherto waterlogged useless, though potentially fertile land, to be cultivated, the introduction of improved seeds, fertilisers, implements and lastly, motor driven vehicles eased the lot of those who worked the land.

The wealth of the islanders lay in their cattle, whose export provided the main source of income. Sheep were kept not as an export, but for their wool (for local weaving) and mutton.

The traditional activities of farming, fishing and forestry, with farming predominating, now employ a greater proportion of Mull's working population than in the Hebrides as a whole, 297 in all in 1986, of whom 185 were in agriculture. At the same time unemployment stood at 7% of the total population, low in comparison with figures elsewhere in Scotland, reflecting the high proportion of elderly and retired people in the island.

Many farmers themselves undertake the whole running of their holding, where the size of the farm or lack of capital cannot justify the expense of hiring labour. More than half the holdings are under 20 acres (8ha), with in most cases the addition of rough hill grazings.

There has been a slow decline in farming, in spite of more intensive management practices. The number of holdings declined from 241 in 1969 to 223 in 1984, with a reduction in the numbers of cattle and sheep.

The Mull farmer has an uphill fight against the encroachment of forestry plantings on grazing lands, the spread of rampant bracken, high transport charges to and from the island, while the climate inhibits the growth of enough fodder to make the island self-supporting. Agriculture is kept 'stringing along' on subsidies. Most of the little trim crofts, like the dozen or so around Tobermory, have been abandoned and lost to bracken and scrub over the last 50 years.

CROFTING

In the agricultural economy of Mull crofting plays only a small part, compared with the thriving crofting communities in Lewis, Harris and Skye, There were in 1970 only 31 crofting holdings: 1 in the north, 1 in the central area and 29 in the Ross of Mull. Here the crofts lie between Bunessan and Fionnphort. Lacking the wide machair lands of the real crofting areas, with a cattle and sheep economy rather than a purely agricultural one, Mull never developed as a crofting island.

Even the largest of the crofts can hardly provide a living, and the holder, him or herself, must work long arduous hours lacking the capital to engage a helper. Crofters are obliged to engage in part-time work. Some inshore fishing is carried on, but rather to provide a food supply than to bring in cash.

Crofting is carried on in Mull chiefly by an older generation, and its future prospects are poor unless some form of encouragement is introduced. Crofts as agricultural units may cease to exist, now the crofter-occupiers can become crofter-owner-occupiers with powers of disposal. If Mull develops as a holiday island, land of this type may become a new and valuable asset for the crofters.

Highland cattle were originally the small, black, hardy breed known as kyloes, which were particularly adapted to the Highlands and Islands through their ability to thrive on the natural coarse grasses of that environment, even on a certain kind of seaweed found along the shores, where other breeds could hardly find a living. They became the main source of cash for crofters and farmers. In the year 1809 there were 8,000 cattle in Mull, of which about one fifth were sold annually along with 700 brought over from the surrounding islands. Their shaggy coats protected them in the damp climate, and with their sturdy frames and restless dispositions they fared better on the open range than in confinement. The passing of the Enclosures Act early in the eighteenth century and the building of walls (that did not happen in Mull until later in the century) restricted grazings along the traditional drove roads of the mainland, and cattle now diverted on to the harder military roads were sometimes shod to protect their hooves. The importance of the cattle trade was recognised in the fact that during the Disarming Act that followed the Jacobite uprising, drovers were allowed to carry arms for protection against cattle-raiders.

Competition from home and abroad and the intensification of sheep grazings during the nineteenth century saw a retraction in the cattle economy, in spite of advances in scientific breeding and feeding since 1800. In 1814 there were between 80 and 100 breeding cows in the two small off-shore islands of Staffa and Gometra. The owner, MacDonald of Staffa, was a famous cattle-breeder and progressive land-owner, who in 1815 sold a herd of three-year-olds at an average price of 14 guineas. In the same year he sold for 130 guineas a bull for which he had earlier refused an offer of 200 guineas, and similar top prices for other animals. Even allowing for depreciation, such prices were astronomical in their day and reflect the quality of his stock.

Early in the nineteenth century cattle-owners began to crossbreed the kyloe with selected mainland strains in an effort to produce a larger-boned animal carrying more beef, which still retained the characteristics of the original kyloe. The resultant breed is the now well-known shaggy Highland animal, with colourations shading from cream to dark reddish brown, with the rare appearance of the original black. Experiments in cross-breeding Highland with Beef Shorthorn cattle in the island of Luing, south of Oban, have produced the new Luing breed, registered in 1965. Hardy, docile, well-wintering in the open, as well as quicker maturing, and able to graze freely above the 1000ft (305m) contour, it is ideally suited to Mull, where it has been successfully introduced. Mull now supports just under four thousand head of cattle.

SHEEP

The indigenous Mull sheep were akin to the Soay sheep, often four horned, small animals yielding only a quarter of the products of the heavier mainland breeds. They were valueless to the eighteenth-century crofters as cash-earning exports. By the end of the 18th century, Cheviot and black-faced flocks were widespread in Mull, superseding the indigenous stock by 1810 as the landlords began to turn over land to the more profitable use of leasing to incoming flockmasters. In 1843 the parish of Torosay alone realised £17,500 from the wool crop.

This intensification of sheep grazing during the nineteenth century not only exacerbated the rate of emigration amongst evicted and unemployed crofters and their families, but ultimately destroyed the cattle grazing lands which became seriously over-cropped and fouled. Grazing sheep also destroyed seedlings and prevented the regeneration of wood-lands. In the end deserted sheep lands became infested with bracken and rabbit warrens or reverted to heather and sour boglands. In 1984 there were 60,000 sheep in Mull, mostly black-faced, of which 20,000 are exported annually. Although this trade is important to the economy of the island, a better balance between sheep and cattle would, it is believed, be more profitable.

PONIES

Hill ponies, a small type of garron, used to be bred in Mull. They were used for carrying loads, creels of peats for instance, and for deer stalking. These ponies were famed for their endurance, believed to have been derived from a strain of Andalusian pony landed from an Armada ship in Tobermory Bay. When Mr J. H. Munro Mackenzie acquired Calgary estate in 1884 he took up the breeding of this type of pony. Calgary ponies became a nationally known breed, with champions unbeaten in the show-ring and wins at Championships and agricultural shows. One fine pony was sold to King Edward VII for £100, an enormous price in the early twentieth century. Many were sold, too, to go overseas. Few ponies have been raised since the 1920s, although a new interest in riding and pony-trekking may lead to a revival of interest in pony breeding in Mull.

THE FUTURE OF FARMING

If farming is to maintain its importance in Mull's economy, several problems must be solved. Some are external, such as the vagaries of the beef trade, Common Market controls, or attempts by our own government to ameliorate the island's ills by legislation. Within the island there are the inherited attitude of the farmers, lack of capital, lack of inducement for young folk to remain on the island, and misuse of land.

One suggestion lies in an expansion of cattle breeding. To echo Fraser Darling, Mull is cattle country equal to the best in the land. The best use of the land would be the rearing of large numbers of good quality stock for fattening on the more lush grazings in the South. Mull's soil lends itself to the improvement of grasslands. The bringing about of this would involve drastic changes in the island, the attitude of the government and the practical use of land. At present a sheep economy predominates, but it is a vicious circle for the small farmer or crofter in a small holding; with little capital to invest, he cannot afford to improve the quality of his stock. Subsidies, on which he depends, might be better related to land improvement, fertilising, fencing, and selective breeding.

Extension of the arable areas and lost cattle grazings would ease the age-long problem of providing winter fodder, and private experiments along these lines have been successful. Livestock production was increased by 50 per cent and more prior to the mid-1960s by the small number of large farms and estates which could afford the project. The authorities concerned with the future well-being of Mull should seriously consider a state-assisted scheme based on the principles of the improvemets already shown to be successful, to benefit the ambitious but under-capitalised stock-raiser, to help the general economy of the island and, with it, that of the country as a whole. At the same time the farmers would have to be willing to collaborate in necessary reorganisation of holdings, and the interests of those unable to maintain larger holdings.

The findings of an investigation carried out in the mid-1960s into Mull's stock-raising potential, and quoted in the *Mull Survey* of 1965, are impressive. They suggest that principles successfully applied between 1960 and 1964 could be adopted as a long-term government policy on the island. On the basis of an area of 21,000 acres (8,500ha), (assumed to be an economic unit of land which could be improved with government aid) the outlay in improvements estimated in 1965, less grants, is shown below. The figures for 1986, which are also shown, do not include government grants, because with changes in official policy many units are now ineligible. Those that are eligible obtain 30 per cent of the gross cost.

	1965 £	1986 £
5,000 acres (2,000ha) ploughed, rotovated, reseeded, fertilised and slagged @ £35 per acre (£120 per acre in 1986)	175,000	600,000
16,000 acres (6,500ha) limed, slagged and surface-seeded @ £15 per acre (£186 per acre in 1986)	240,000	2,976,000
100 miles of fencing @ £5,000 per mile (£2.20 per yard in 1986)	50,000	387,200
	465,000	3,963,200

It was estimated that this improved area would support 5,500 cattle (a 140 per cent increase on the number of cattle grazed there before the experiment) or 30 per cent more lambs, in each case with better breeding quality. A rise in productivity on this scale for a single grant of this figure could not have been found by the government in the industrial world.

Afforestation is frequently a cause for controversy, for there is a conflict of interests between the farmer, the sporting-estate owner and the forester. In Mull the Forestry Commission is now the largest land-owning body and the plantations are steadily expanding.

The first land was taken over by the commission in 1924 on the Aros estate, followed between 1928 and 1930 by areas at Lettermore (Loch Frisa) and Fishnish (near Craignure), a total of 1,700 acres (688ha). Post-war expansion of the forests started in 1952 and by the autumn of 1967 the commission had increased its holdings to 38,000 acres (15,500ha), of which the Department of Agriculture managed 16,000 acres (6,500ha) on behalf of the commission. Of the remaining area, nearly 10,000 acres (4,000ha) were under trees, with plantings amounting to 1,000 acres (400ha) a year. A proportion of the total holdings – under rocks and in gullies and bogs, for instance – is unusable. In 1984, 15 per cent of Mull was under trees, with planned annual plantings of 620–740 acres (250–300ha). Private plantings are estimated at about 400 acres (160ha) per annum and, with the present government policy of favouring the private sector, this may become increasingly important.

The plantations are chiefly of Sitka spruce (57.6 per cent) which has proved to be the most adaptable, and Japanese larch (12.3 per cent). Larch is often planted for aesthetic purposes and to form windbreaks. The plantations are healthy, with few traces of disease that cannot readily be eliminated. During severe gales there is sometimes loss through wind-throw, but on a surprisingly small scale. Red deer and sheep will nibble the tender growing points of young trees as well as the bark; a species of the common vole peculiar to Mull, will destroy very young trees by ring-barking, though this damage is confined so far to the Ardmore plantations. The cost of essential fencing for young plantations is high. Wire netting of 1¼in (3cm) mesh was formerly required to exclude the hordes of rabbits that infested the island, but their near-extermination by myxomatosis in the early 1950s made this requirement less essential, although the rabbit population is increasing again. The Mull Forest is now nearing full production as planned. The commission now produces about 14,000 cubic yards (11,000m³) of timber annually, a quantity which will steadily increase as plantations mature. About half of the production goes to the local sawmill at Pennyghael, the

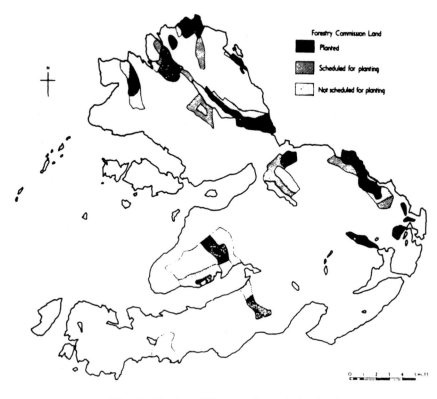

The distribution of Forestry Commission land

rest leaving the island as logs. One developing problem is the use of heavy timber lorries on the minor weight-restricted Mull roads.

The steady employment that the Forestry Commission provides is greatly welcomed in Mull. Permanent work is assured for a labour force of over fifty foresters and twenty casual road-makers and workers. A basic wage, augmented by 40–50 per cent piece-work, provides a reasonable standard of living. The commission has also brought new amenities to the island, in the form of new houses and roads. Housing is provided for the forestry workers, as well as for the agricultural holdings (now nine in number). There is one chief forestry officer, based at Aros, with deputies at Dervaig, Kinloch and Craignure. Little increase in the labour force is likely; expansion will mostly be met by mechanised techniques.

The commission and the Department of Agriculture work jointly to preserve some balance of land use, while local interests are kept in mind by the Red Deer Commission, and the Nature Conservancy. The Forestry Commission therefore is endeavouring to compromise with the interests of all these agencies. Nevertheless, some over-hasty plantations have been made on valuable agricultural lands, at Aros, Lettermore, Gruline, Tiroran, Kilfinichen, Fishnish and Ardtun, which have aroused some bitter criticisms in Mull farming circles.

11   *INDUSTRIES PAST AND PRESENT*

The island's natural resources for economic development, other than pastoral farming and forestry, are very limited indeed. Of the industries developed in the past the burning of seaweed (kelp) probably had the greatest social impact, coinciding as it did with a large increase in population. Tourism may yet play an important part in changing some of the economy of the island and its landscape, and indeed its beneficial impact is making itself felt. But the development of new light industry, with necessary financial investment in the island, is probably an essential accompaniment to a more rational policy for modern pastoral farming and forestry, aiming towards the stabilisation of Mull's economy and population. But even in a time of national ecomonic recovery, industry would still be inhibited by the very insularity of Mull and the disadvantages already outlined.

THE KELP INDUSTRY

The kelp of the Western Isles is the *Laminaria* seaweed, the 'Tangle of the Isles', which grows in vast beds, with long thick stems and large glossy leaves, especially on the rocky western coasts of the islands. The beds are half exposed at low tide, and there occurs a natural thinning of the weed, especially in late autumn, when immense quantities of the tangle are torn from the sea-floor and tossed up on the beaches. Originally the name 'kelp' was applied not to the weed itself, but to the alkaline ash produced after burning. In the early farming economy kelp, which is relatively rich in potash, was of great importance, for it was used as manure on the light, shelly

174

machair lands, and with even more beneficial effects on soft mossy ground. In addition to kelp, every available variety of seaweed was used for this purpose.

The exploitation of both the kelp and the people came when a new industry was developed which was profitable to the lairds but which led many of the crofters, who were by the nature of the island confined to live around its shores, into the harsh life of kelp burning. The industry originated in France at the end of the seventeenth century, when it was discovered that the alkaline ash, known then as *Soude de Varich*, obtained from calcined seaweeds, was an effective substitute for barilla. Although it was introduced into Scotland in the middle of the eighteenth century, and had a small measure of commercial success at the time of the American War of Independence, the rise and decline of kelp is more associated with the Napoleonic wars, which coincided with a time when the addition of the potato to the islanders' diet in fact led to an increase in population and a ready supply of labour. The harvesting of what amounted to an export crop that had no part in the food economy contributed little to their welfare, for tenancy rights were often involved in the remuneration for their work. However, additional wages were usually paid to the workers, which although low according to modern standards were a new and valuable source of income for a community where hard cash was scarce. The crofters were sometimes accused of neglecting their lands by diverting too much kelp to the new industry instead of spreading it on the food-producing ground.

Kelp, when burnt, produces an impure alkali, which can be used in the manufacture of glass, soap and bleaching agents, and in the processing of linen. It was originally imported largely from Spain. Twenty tons of tangle would be needed to produce a ton of kelp ash. When the Napoleonic wars were over and the blockade was lifted, barilla could again be imported; the kelp industry of the Western Isles collapsed, with far-reaching social consequences.

The collecting and burning of kelp was very hard, uncongenial work and – being exploitative of the crofters' labour – was also degrading. The work involved much hardship and physical endurance, and in fact the incidence of rheumatism in the Hebrides is reported in the *Statistical Account* of 1845 to have been at its highest during the intensive period of the kelp industry. The plants were collected at low water and carried up to the drying and burning area in creels on the back of every member of the family old enough to help, or on ponies, or in carts, according to the nature of the shore. After drying, the kelp was burned in kilns or trenches, or between carefully arranged layers of peat, where it melted down into a kind of slag. It was a skilled task, requiring a close watch to be kept on the temperature of the burning mass. A close watch was also kept, later, by the buyers of the finished product, for unscrupulous workers sometimes inserted stones or sand to make up the weight, affecting both quality and price. In Mull some of the lairds threatened that any tenant found guilty of the practice would be instantly evicted from his holding and prosecuted.

Mull produced about 600 tons of kelp ash annually – 8.5 per cent of the total production of the West Highland region. At peak prosperity this brought in £12,000 to £15,000 in hard cash to the island. The alkaline content of Mull seaweed was high, but its distribution was so affected by the nature of the rocky shores that the actual output was well below the potential. 'Kelp' included other forms of seaweed in addition to the tangle, which, although bulky, did not yield such high-quality ash as 'button wrack', described in the *Statistical Account* of 1795 as being the best to use for burning, 'unless the price is very high'. The chief centre lay around Loch na Keal (that is, Gribun, Ulva and Inch Kenneth), with other corners of the island adding their quota.

The profits belonged to the landlords. In order to attract workers they set aside land and divided it into what became known as 'crofts', with common grazings. Whole families who engaged in this seasonal work could earn as much as £8 in the year, a very welcome cash addition to the produce of their crofts. Rents in kelp-burning areas soared: in the twenty years ending in 1791 the rents paid to the proprietors of the parish of Kilfinichen and Kilviceon alone rose from £961 to £2,711.

By 1825, however, the imports of barilla had been restored and the import duty was repealed. By 1834 the price of kelp was down to £3 per ton. Workers suffered through loss of earnings; but some landlords, who had come to depend on this new and easy source of income to finance a wider and more luxurious way of living, were faced with ruin. This desperation for hard cash was one of the factors leading to the land clearances and the introduction of the more profitable sheep.

The *Statistical Account* of 1845 summarises the contemporary situation:

> The manufacture has entirely disappeared, with the exception of a very little made at Innis Kenneth and Gribun. Before barilla was allowed to enter our market duty free, and thereby exclude the kelp, there were no less than 150 tons annually manufactured in this parish [Kilfinichen and Kilviceon], and of course it, in common with the Highlands in general, has felt the loss . . . In previous years this manufacture employed and gave bread to many thousands in the Highlands and Islands, and the price it drew . . . being circulated through the Kingdom at large, kept the money at home, which now goes to enrich the foreigner at the poor Highlander's expense; a measure of policy which cannot be too strongly condemned – for whether it arose from ignorance on the part of the government, or from any other cause, the Highlands have since the admission of duty free barilla and other substances, presented scenes of much distress, bankruptcy and poverty.

Perhaps Highlanders – and Scotsmen as a whole – will be forgiven for suggesting that government policy seems to have changed little since then.

Mull did not share in the modern industry that developed producing sodium alginates from seaweeds, which started up in two places in the Hebrides in the 1960s, the product being processed at Girvan, in Ayrshire. Kelp, bladder-wrack and brown ware are collected, dried, crushed, bagged and sent in this compact form to the factory, where they are chemically processed to yield alginates, a general name given to purified chemicals obtained from seaweeds. There are many uses for alginates: for controlling the viscosity of food products, as a gelling agent for various desserts, in pharmaceutical products, for the formation of surface films, even for controlling the rate of flow in welding materials.

INDUSTRIES PAST AND PRESENT

Mull is reported to have too low a concentration of seaweeds to justify setting up a collecting and drying plant, and certainly the configuration of the coast – as in the days of the kelp industry – would reduce any potential crop.

DISTILLING

In Mull, as well as in so many other remote districts, there was a large undercover industry right up to the early nineteenth century. This was one industry that flourished on remoteness and bad communications – the illicit distilling of whisky. Distilling was carried on with impunity in such wild and remote corners as Carsaig, Burg, Lochbuie, Loch Ba and Treshnish. For example, the foundations of a large still can be examined at the entrance to a deep, dry cave below the old township of Crakaig, west of Torloisk. It lies at the base of the lower cliff, just above the reach of the highest tides, the only approach from inland being down a steep cleft or gully in the cliff. A zigzag bridle-path has been built down this, starting cunningly at the outer edge of the cliff above, which was passable for ponies carrying loads of peat and grain one way, and kegs of spirits the other.

The staves of old kegs still lie at the inner end of the cave. A tiny stream was diverted to drop across the front of the cave just a few feet from the still, conveniently close for cooling the 'worm' from the distillation pot – or *poit dhubh* (the black pot) as it was called – which was most probably made, along with the rest of the plumbing, by the blacksmith who lived at that time in the village above. This sat over a furnace, a hemispherical hollow 8ft (2.4m) in diameter by 3ft (90cm) deep, with an air duct led in from below, the whole enclosed in a circular platform of rocks 15ft (4.6m) in diameter. Outside the cave are the remains of a turf wall which would have been built high enough to hide the reflection of the furnace from passing boats. This writer once lit a fire of driftwood in the furnace and watched how the dense smoke pouring out of the cave seemed to cling to the face of the cliff and dissipate. On the raised beach 120ft (37m) above the cave there are many bright green bracken-infested patches of former cultivation, where much of the grain was doubtless grown to supply the malt for the still. The whole project was cleverly designed and virtually undetectable.

The cove in front of the cave had a channel which had been cleared of boulders to allow boats to be run in. From here early last century the still was being operated by the forefathers of a local family who rowed and sailed all the way across to Ireland in their open fishing boat to sell some of their produce. Mull people must certainly have had the art of producing high-quality whisky, when they could compete profitably in the land of the poteen.

Another still of the same type, but much smaller, takes up one room in a tiny two-roomed cot-house, one of half a dozen or so lost and forgotten in a hazel wood not fifty yards from the main road in the north of Mull. A burn was diverted to supply the cooling water.

Illicit distilling ended as an undercover industry in 1823, when legislation was passed to allow the owner of the ground on which a still was found to be punished heavily along with the operators. Up to then the landowners, benefitting indirectly from the extra cash raised from spirits, were on the side of the producers.

The end of what could be called an illegal cottage industry saw the start of what was to become a lucrative Highland industry and an important source of government revenue. Whisky distilling was legalised in the Highlands and subjected to duty in line with the system that had hitherto been operating in the Lowland distilleries. It was in 1823 that a distillery was started up at Tobermory, at Ledaig, at the foot of the Eas Brae (Cataract Hill) where the Tobermory Burn, tumbling steeply down from the upland moors and peat bogs, enters the sea. The quality of the water was found to be excellent, which is one of the vital factors in producing a good whisky, and indeed a malt whisky of fine blending quality was subsequently produced here.

The Tobermory distillery was built for two local farming brothers, MacKell by name, and the construction was carried out by John Sinclair of Lochaline. In 1874 it was taken over by the Glasgow company of John Hopkins & Co Ltd and by

1880 it was producing the famous 'Old Mull' registered brand of whisky. Between 1900 and 1920 the average annual output was nearly 250,000 gallons (1 million litres) of malt whisky. Taken over by the Distillers Company Ltd in 1917, what was now a subsidiary company was closed down in 1924, partly as being uneconomic in comparison with distilleries on the mainland, notably that of the Glenlivet group just south of the Moray Firth, home area of Highland whisky production; partly through a fall in demand through Prohibition in America.

Nearly fifty years later, in 1972, a new company, Ledaig Distillery (Tobermory) Ltd, took over the distillery – 11,000sq ft (1,000m^2) of production space and 14,000sq ft (1,300m^2) of warehousing – and re-equipped and modernised it at a cost of £350,000. About fifteen jobs were provided at comparatively high wages, this in an island where at the time 38 males were out of work out of an employable number of 523. Production began in 1972, reached 200,000 gallons (900,000 litres) the first year and trebled by the end of 1975, using the same source of water.

Misled by the seemingly limitless demand for whisky then, the company over-expanded and then had to suspend business, a blow to local employment. There followed a period of speculation as to the future of the distillery, with interest in a takeover being shown by foreign business interests from as far away as Japan. However, in 1979 a Yorkshire business-man, Mr Stewart C. Jowett, formed a company, The Tobermory Distillers Limited, which acquired the distillery lock, stock and barrel, and prepared to market what was called the 'Tobermory' blend, as well as a straight malt. The administration of the company was highly experienced and aimed for quality rather than quantity. Unfortunately, the recession in the Scottish whisky trade resulted in a cessation of operations in 1984, which, it is hoped, will be temporary.

In 1982 a new liqueur whisky, with cream and honey, was first produced on Mull by a retired businessman, Mr John Bartholomew. Although production was at first on a very small scale, the demand for the liqueur, known as Columba Cream, exceeded all expectations and developed into the family business of John Murray & Company (Mull) Ltd. The production centre has been moved to the mainland for greater convenience.

FISHING

In 1789, as a result of several factors – industrial expansion on the west coast of the Scottish mainland, the urgency of finding work for the expanding population, and the difficulties of obtaining salt privately under the new tax laws – a fish marketing agency was set up at Tobermory. This was founded by the British Society for Encouraging Fisheries through the efforts of the then Duke of Argyll. The plan was to establish sixty settlers, including a few experienced men from the East Coast, each with 12 acres (4.9ha) of land, a common outrun on the hill, and rights of peat-cutting.

However, although Tobermory offered a good enough haven for the fishing fleets, it was too near the commercial facilities of Oban to compete in the fish market. A good deal of reclamation of the foreshore was carried out, which allowed an extension of the main street across the burn, and the erection of a number of new buildings. Those improvements were of lasting benefit to the town, some local trading developed, and for a time a small boat-building business was carried on.

Fishermen from Tobermory and the whole of Mull had to face strong competition from larger and better-equipped boats from the East Coast, manned by professional fishermen whose livelihood depended entirely on fishing. The West Coast fishing was for subsistence rather than commerce and the crofter fished for his family, using outdated methods and equipment. There was further competition from foreign boats, which were exploiting the West Coast from as early as 1632, and which continue to do so to the present day.

About the time of this Tobermory venture the Duke of Argyll tried to establish a similar scheme on his own lands on the Sound of Iona but the project failed after struggling for a few years.

There is no lack of variety in the fish to be caught around

Mull: herring, cod, ling, mackerel, saithe, lythe, rockfish, flounder, plaice, sole, turbot, skate and others, which, however, are sought more by the commercial fishermen using organised methods.

A profitable line in sprat fishing was introduced by one observant local fisherman. Observing fine scales on the wide meshes of some of his nets and suspecting the presence of shoals of sprats, he tried a few experimental 'shots' with sprat equipment, with good results.

In Mull the number of registered fishing boats rose from 18, with 39 fishermen, to 32 and 56 respectively in 1982. Some of the fishermen work part time. These boats concentrate on high-value catches of shellfish, and the value of landings of scallops, prawns, crabs, lobsters, mussels and whelks has risen from £320,000 in 1978 to £709,000 in 1982. Although half of this can be attributed to boats from outside Mull, the industry has a significant place in the economy.

In Tobermory the local fishermen have acquired the rights to the Old Pier, which is convenient for landings and storage of equipment, although boats are grounded at low tide. Repairs to MacBrayne's pier completed in 1985 benefit fishing boats, especially larger ones of deeper draught.

Tough, endurable, finer nylon has replaced the former cordage for nets, eliminating much of the constant examination and repairs formerly required.

One thriving industry is lobster fishing, and Mull contributes a substantial proportion to the West Coast production. The lobsters are of excellent quality. Alick (Ban) MacDougall, to whom reference has already been made, fished for lobsters round the coasts of Calliach and Treshnish, and the quality of his catches was so high that up to the time of his death he had a firm order from the Cunard Line to supply it with as many lobsters as possible for use on the *Queens* on the North Atlantic run. Careful packing and express delivery ensured that the lobsters carried well, and the inevitably high freightage was offset by the good prices obtained.

The lobster pot, or creel, is of simple construction and the frame can easily be home-made, or manufactured nowadays with a metal frame. It is no more than a flat board on which is lashed a heavy, flat stone as a sinker, with semicircular hazel withies fixed to support a net of stout cord or nylon, with a small section which can be untied for inserting bait or removing the catch – which can sometimes include anything from conger eels to shellfish as well as the lobster. Entrance is by two opposed funnel-like openings, one of which is always invitingly exposed no matter how the creel is lying. The creels are dropped in water between 5 and 20 fathoms (9–36m) deep, near rocks, in lots of half a dozen upwards, connected to the one rope which is marked by a floating buoy.

Loss of tackle can be serious when a storm blows up with a heavy ground swell; worse still is the wholesale scooping up of 'everything that crawls' (as one exasperated lobster fisher described it) by large foreign boats, which can smother a bay with modern gear and clean it out in a night, ignoring the regulations governing minimum size (9in/23cm) within which our fishers must operate. Add to this the illegal trawling in-shore by large craft which goes on in the absence of sufficient government patrol vessels of proper design, and some picture can be formed of what the crofter-fisher – and the home fishing fleet – is up against.

One of the largest lobsters ever caught off the British Isles ws taken in Calgary Bay, below Craig-a'Chaisteal, in the 1920s by Alick MacDougall and his cousin. Measuring 3ft 1in (94m) from its tail to the tip of its feelers, the span of its claws was 2ft 10in (86cm) and the circumference of a claw 13in (33cm). Weighing over 12lb (5.4kg), it sold for £5, and was on show for months in the window of a leading Glasgow fishmonger. Too large to enter and too greedy to let go, this monster clung to the creel as it was drawn up to the surface, where a rope was quickly passed round it.

Another profitable small-scale business is salmon fishing. Certain stretches of coastal waters are let to salmon fishers, whose nets are staked across the tidal paths followed by the salmon round the coasts, especially off headlands and river mouths. The floating nets consist of two long leaders 12ft (3.7m) deep kept taut between two upright stakes – anchored in the seabed – by the action of the tides against the line of floats above and the anchors below. Salmon come up against the leaders, which are at right angles to the path of the fish, and follow them until they reach a central 'bag' in the nets into which they swim through a narrow vertical slit designed on the non-return principle.

The boat is drawn up against the upper edge of the bag which is then manhandled to the surface; a detachable section is opened, and the salmon taken out, killed, and stored in the boat. On shore the fish are weighed and packed in boxes, taken by van to Craignure to catch the last car-ferry of the day, and conveyed to Glasgow overnight where they arrive next morning in fine condition at the fish market. The high freight charge is to some extent offset by the good prices received.

Seals can cause costly damage by tearing the nets to get at the trapped salmon, allowing many to escape and leaving others badly mangled. This is a serious financial problem for salmon fishers running what can be a precarious business during a very short summer season. While seals have their place, any increase in their numbers would have serious repercussions. There is also the risk of losing nets when basking sharks become accidentally entangled, to say nothing of wholesale destruction by sudden storms.

The Herring Industry Board has suggested that a fish-drying plant could be set up in Mull to handle surplus fish from the Oban–Mallaig area, but no progress has been made with this idea. The White Fish Authority has been conducting experiments in fish farming at one or two centres elsewhere – that is, experiments in the rearing of fish from selected eggs or hatched fish, particularly flatfish such as Dover sole, and feeding them to marketable size. This has proved to be a successful experiment, and as time goes on it might well become a crofter-fisher industry of the future, using submerged cages conveniently sited in sea-lochs and other sheltered coastal inlets. Mull would be an excellent area for such a venture.

In August 1974, after three years of experiment, a retired businessman, Mr Hugh Goldie, who settled in Tobermory, decided that fish farming was commercially viable. Initially as a hobby, he had reared trout fry in tanks in his garden, with a supply of running fresh water from the little burn that flowed through the village here. Operations were transferred to more suitable premises beside another burn at Port a'Choit, beyond MacBrayne's pier. Here, in large tanks of running water, and with automatic feeding, salmon, brown-, rainbow- and steelhead-trout grow to a length of 5–6in (13–15cm). Sea-water is pumped up from the sea below and gradually introduced to replace the fresh water, and in due course the fish can be safely moved into cages of close-mesh nets suspended in Tobermory Bay just off the Aros Burn, where the salinity of the water is reduced. Other cages are sited in the fresh water of Aros Lake. While trout can safely be moved from sea or saline water directly into fresh, the change from fresh to salt must be gradual to allow fish to adjust to the reduced oxygen content.

In the cages up to a hundred thousand fish are growing rapidly on a diet of minced fish offal compacted and frozen into blocks, which melt slowly and release a steady supply of food, avoiding the wasteful practice of scattering unfrozen food. When they reach the marketable size of 6–8oz (170–230g) they are removed for sale in the Tobermory Fish Shop, where they find a ready market, especially in the island's hotels. Smoked trout or salmon is something of a delicacy.

Brown trout are also supplied for restocking the Mishnish Lochs and Loch Torr. On Loch Torr, rainbow-trout are also released, some of them up to 6lb (2.7kg) in weight, providing some exciting angling. Rainbow-trout develop faster, but have a much shorter lifespan than brown trout.

By 1984 similar enterprises had started up at Gruline, on Loch na Keal, and Loch Spelve. In the last named there is also the rearing of oysters and mussels, with an oyster farm at Pennyghael.

MILLING

Up to the middle of the nineteenth century there were at least six sizeable water-mills actively working, each producing about 300 bolls of meal in the year (a boll is approximately

185

168lb/76kg). In 1892 there were still two oatmeal mills working, one in the Ross of Mull and one in the north. Water-mills in Mull were used also by the grain-growers in the island of Tiree to grind the abundant harvests grown in this 'land of corn', as the name is said to mean. Mills were owned and run by the landowners as profitable sidelines. Long ago the people were forbidden in some places to use their own small hand-querns, as this would have deprived the mills of custom.

There were two types of mill: the 'clack' mill, built directly over the water, which turned the wheel and delivered power through a vertical shaft and gearing; and the more conventional type where water led along a mill lade poured on to the flanges of a large revolving wheel which transmitted power along a horizontal shaft. The introduction of cheap foreign grain to Britain during the nineteenth century and of commercial milling sited at or near the arrival ports led to the availability of flour and oatmeal for import to the island, both cheaper and more attractively presented, although, as now-adays, losing something of their nourishing value in the processing. There was an inevitable decline in the local grain trade and milling. Where formerly there were many small mills throughout the island, not a trace now remains except in place names, such as *Tom a'Mhuillin* (the mound by the mill – at Tobermory) and faint traces of old mill lades.

A small industry connected with milling was the cutting and finishing of millstones, some of which measured up to 5ft (1.5m) in diameter. This was carried out at Gribun, where there is an outcrop, just above high-water mark, of a pebbly siliceous gritstone of Triassic age, which is of high quality for the purpose. It lies 150yd (140m) west of the shed and garage of the Inch Kenneth ferry; one defective millstone can still be seen lying in the bed from which it was being cut. Twenty or thirty millstones were made annually, and most were exported to the islands, from which boats or smacks came right in-shore for loading.

THE TOURIST INDUSTRY

The tourist industry is now a major part of the Mull economy, valued at several million pounds annually, and the organisation to support it has kept pace into the 1980s. The accessibility of Mull, yet its refreshing Hebridean atmosphere of remoteness, have established it firmly as a holiday island, yet it is comparatively unspoilt. Accommodation has expanded and now meets the demand: in fact, it is suggested that this be still further improved rather than extended. In 1986 there were 22 hotels and guest houses in Mull and two in Iona, and around 200 houses offering 'self-catering' or bed and breakfast.

Hotels and guest-houses have been brought up to modern standards. At Craignure a luxury sixty-bedroom hotel costing £300,000 opened in the early 1970s, sponsored by the Highland Development Board and run by the Scottish Highland Hotels Group. The project received only qualified approval from Mull people, who considered that such a sum might have been more effectively spent on the improvement of a range of existing establishments.

At all the centres there are restaurants and bar lunches to tide the sightseer over a long day. There is an efficient information centre in Main Street, Tobermory, run by the Oban, Mull and District Tourist Association where excellent guidebooks and advice can be obtained. There is a youth hostel in Tobermory.

The industry is of course greatly helped by its lines of communication with the mainland. Here is an analysis of the total passenger and vehicle traffic carried on the Lochaline/Fishnish and Oban/Craignure ferries between the mainland and Mull:

OBAN/CRAIGNURE AND LOCHALINE/FISHNISH FERRY TRAFFIC

Year	Passengers	Motor Vehicles
1951	24,000	454
1960	36,000	1,131
1963	43,000	1,514
1964*	68,000	5,344
1967**	199,000	17,496
1968	233,000	20,483
1979†	341,294	65,156

187

1980[†]	318,613	59,845
1981[†]	301,799	57,727
1982[†]	307,693	60,161
1983[†]	345,382	66,121
1984[†]	381,900	73,500
1985[†]	387,200	76,600

[*] Craignure Pier opened
[**] Roll-on roll-off installed
[†] Fishnish Ferry figures included

The above selected figures clearly show the benefits conferred on an island community by improved communications, as well as the upsurge of a tourist industry. There was a small but steady decline between 1979 and 1982 attributable to the national recession, increasing petrol prices and the increasing attraction of holidays abroad, but since then the figures have improved through more intensive marketing and publicity. It is now not unusual in July and August for the earlier car ferries of the day to land over six hundred passengers on each trip to Craignure, where they are met by a fleet of coaches to convey them on sight-seeing trips round the island, and to their destinations at Salen, Tobermory and the Ross of Mull.

The island provides something for every taste, from research to entertainment, geology, archaeology, ornithology, botany – the fields to explore are many and varied. For golfers there is Tobermory's short but picturesque and challenging course, or at the new course at Craignure; and even Iona can offer golf! Anglers can explore the lochs and rivers for salmon and sea-trout in season, as well as brown- and rainbow-trout. The eel is the only other freshwater fish in Mull. Sea angling is excellent and record specimens have been taken. Boats can be hired privately or for parties at Tobermory and other centres, either for fishing or cruising, for example, to the unforgettable Treshnish Islands and Staffa described later. As mentioned earlier, the area is a paradise for yachters. Skin-diving, sea-bathing, pony-trekking – all are available.

There are plenty of craft shops throughout the island, some

surprisingly isolated but in places of natural beauty. Metal and shell work, paintings (there is a residential school of painting), wool and fabrics, crooks and sticks, can all be found. There are regular concerts and ceilidhs, agricultural and flower shows, a week-long musical festival in April and a major motor-car rally in October.

Duart Castle, 3 miles east of Craignure, home of Lord Maclean, chief of the clan, is open to the public; a wonderful old building with a hundred rooms round a central courtyard, whose romantic history goes back to the thirteenth century. Just over a mile from Craignure stands the mansion-house of Torosay – Torosay Castle – a family home built in the Scottish baronial style by David Bryce in 1856, with magnificent Italian terraced gardens and a statue walk laid out by Sir John Lorimer in 1899. It, too, is open to the public, with the unique advantage of being linked with Craignure by the only passenger railway in the Hebrides! Tens of thousands of visitors visit these buildings annually.

ANCILLARY OCCUPATIONS

Reference is made in other chapters to quarrying and peat cutting, as well as to iron-working. Most settlements had their own blacksmith or iron-worker, descendants of the craftsmen who forged and shaped the tools of war when those were in greater demand than agricultural implements. The word *gobhainn* (anglicised to 'gowan') is the Gaelic name for a blacksmith; it appears in many place-names, marking the former existence of a smithy, but the smiths themselves have, like the water-mills, disappeared except for a few workshops run as a sideline to cater for odd repairs. There is an excellent repair garage and service station at Tobermory, with smaller ones at Salen, Craignure and Pennyghael.

In 1971 a Shell/BP oil depot opened at Craignure where oil can be pumped ashore direct from small local tankers. The cost of construction was £65,000. There is capacity for 250,000 gallons (1 million litres). In spite of this facility, as mentioned earlier, the price of petrol in Mull remains at least 10p in excess of that on the nearest point of the mainland.

The arts of weaving and dyeing were well known in the old isolated communities. Heather, crotal (lichen), iris root, bog-myrtle and the bark of certain trees were the chief sources of dyes, but many of the secrets have been lost. In 1789 the Duke of Argyll hoped to develop from this a small industry in yarn- and net-making, but this did not prosper.

As mentioned earlier, excellent craft shops have been established throughout the island selling high-grade articles made in the island. In Tobermory Main Street an old church now houses an excellent display of craft items, overlooked by the attractive rose window. In Iona the rare Iona pebble provides the material for a great variety of jewellery.

DRY-STONE WALLING

This began first in the district of Kirkcudbright, in the Borders country, about 1710, after the passing of the earlier Enclosures Act. In Mull it was introduced in the late eighteenth and early nineteenth centuries to fix the marches between farms and the boundaries of the new estates, to protect arable lands, and grazings containing livestock which had hitherto to be watched or tethered to protect the crops. Some of these dykes were massive; the estate march dykes in particular were often as much as 6ft (1.8m) in height and 3ft (90cm) wide at the base. Heavy rocks used in the building had to be sledged, or carried on two-man hods long distances over rough and hilly ground. One yard of standard 4ft 6in (1.3m) dyke required a ton of stones, and although they were in ample supply, the rough, amorphous basaltic rocks of Mull were harder to work and shape than the sandstones and schistic rocks that could be suitably split in other parts of the country. The craftsmen who built the 'black houses' (whose walls were formed virtually of two high dry-stone dykes built close together with an infilling of peat, etc) easily adapted their skill to the building of dry-stone dykes. In 1820 they worked from 7am to 6pm, walking time extra, for a weekly wage of 4s 6d (22½p), plus an allowance for oatmeal. Today, when old boundary walls become ruinous, they are replaced by the stob and wire fence which has only a short life compared with the 150 years of the durable – but now more expensive dry-stone wall. The quarrying and export of Ross of Mull granite up to the 1920s has been described earlier.

ELECTRICITY

Electricity for public use was first generated in Tobermory in the middle 1920s. A small hydro-electric generating plant was erected below the waterfall halfway down the Eas Brae and driven by water piped down from a small storage tank built on the Tobermory River at Tom a'Mhuillin Bridge. This supply was later augmented by a diesel generating plant which was housed in the then disused distillery buildings. A supply of power from Tobermory was extended to the adjacent district. In 1947 the undertakings at Tobermory were acquired by the North of Scotland Hydro-Electric Board.

Then in 1966 Mull was connected to the mainland grid of the board by two sumbarine cables, one crossing the mile-wide Sound of Mull from Ardtornish (near Lochaline, in Morvern) to Fishnish Bay, just north of Craignure, the other running from Oban, across the island of Kerrera, then crossing the 4 miles under the Firth of Lorne to Grass Point.

The electricity board offered favourable terms to the first consumers when power was brought into their district; later consumers had to pay a very high connection charge unless the power lines passed close to their house. Installation costs in 1970 were £70 for each pole erected. In 1986 this figure had risen to £300, which would make the cost prohibitive for new and outlying consumers. Fortunately, nearly every district in Mull is now well served. The power lines to the north of Mull have been upgraded and in 1986 a supply cable was extended from Langamull, between Dervaig and Calgary, across the seabed to the islands of Coll and Tiree.

SPORTING ESTATES

In Victorian and Edwardian times sporting estates provided some steady employment for gamekeepers, stalkers, boatmen and domestic staffs. An extract from the records of Torosay estate (near Craignure) kindly made available by Mrs Miller illustrates the employment conditions of the time – 30 September 1865:

Servants who are worth keeping and necessary for the place:

Gamekeeper W. Currie £45 a year, pint of milk per day or a cow's grass, and seven tons of coal per annum.
Forester J. McGregor 15s [75p] a week or £40 a year, pint of milk and his bothie (his bed, bedding and fuel). Unmarried. A good servant.
Ploughman J. Campbell £24 a year, milk, house, 6/7 tons of coal. £6.10s [£6.50] in lieu of 6½ bolls of meal and 12 barrels of potatoes per annum. A first-rate man.
Gardener G. Cruickshank 14s [70p] a week; wants 17s [85p]. Milk and bothie. Fuel, say 6 tons coal.
Two Apprentices £5 a year each. £6.10s [£6.50] in lieu of meal.
Milk and their bothie.
Fisherman J. MacKinnon 10s [50p] a week and house. 3 tons coals. (He pays for his milk.) A first-rate boatman and desirable in other ways.
Sawman Sandie Lamont 11s [55p] a week and a house. 3 tons coals. No milk. Attends to gasometer. Boatman on the place.
Dairy or Cow Woman 5s [25p) a week and a room over the bothie.

In those days there was a fair income from the letting of shootings and fishings, but such times have gone. Unless financially independent of their estates, the landowners can barely afford to maintain their houses and policies, let alone grouse moors, shootings and fishings. Some sporting estates have already been made over to the Forestry Commission. Deer farming is a possibility, as there is a steady demand from abroad for venison. However, an estate must be large enough to carry sufficient head of deer to justify the capital expenditure and upkeep of extra staff, and to cover the costs of slaughtering, hygienic storing, disposal of by-products such as bone and horn, and expensive transport.

INDUSTRIES PAST AND PRESENT

MARKET-GARDENING

Market-gardening is carried out in a small way at a number of locations in the island, the most important of which in the north of Mull is Glengorm. In view of the low off-season demand for a small population, the short duration of the tourist season, the uncertainty of the weather, labour difficulties and the high costs of transporting fertilisers in and the products out, it is doubtful whether it is worth while establishing any major marketing scheme, although the soil is fertile enough. Garden produce from the mainland will continue to appear in the shops to meet the balance of seasonal demands.

BANKING

The first bank in the vicinity of Mull was a branch of the Paisley Bank opened in Oban on 8 September 1790. It received rents on account of the Duke of Argyll in exchange for 'receipts payable in Edinburgh at twenty days' currency'.

Although a good deal of Mull's financial affairs are still handled in Oban, Tobermory has for well over a century catered adequately for the banking requirements of the island. Just before the middle of the nineteenth century a branch of the Western Bank was opened in Tobermory, but the office closed down a few years later through the disastrous failure of its esteemed but short-lived parent institution in Glasgow. Its business was taken over in Tobermory in the same year (1857) by the Clydesdale Bank, with its head office in Glasgow. Then early in the twentieth century the North of Scotland and Town and County Bank Ltd opened a branch in Tobermory – its head office was in Aberdeen – and the two offices operated in friendly competition until just after World War II, when these two Scottish banks – by then subsidiaries of the Midland Bank Ltd – amalgamated under the name of Clydesdale Bank Ltd. The businesses of the two Tobermory offices were combined in the premises of the former North of Scotland Bank Ltd, a much more handsone building, and the old Clydesdale Bank office was sold.

INDUSTRIES PAST AND PRESENT

For a year or two around 1878 the Clydesdale Bank ran a sub-office at Salen from its Tobermory office. Then, towards the end of the century, a branch of the National Bank of Scotland Ltd opened in Tobermory, but closed in a year or two. The Royal Bank of Scotland opened there in the 1920s, but closed its office down in 1969. The Clydesdale Bank (now 'plc') serves the island through the medium of its travelling bank – 'The bank on wheels' – that visits centres in the whole island in turn on set week-days.

EMPLOYMENT AND THE FUTURE

Because the island's population is an ageing one and its basic economy is weak, unemployment benefit, social security and retirement pensions play all too large a part in maintaining standards of living in Mull. Many people are glad to retire to the island in financial comfort but others, for lack of opportunity during a lifetime spent there, have been able to make little provision for their later years.

As matters stand, where the island is dependent on its traditional resources no dramatic expansion in its economy is possible. Basically, the new industry of tourism cannot be included in these traditional resources until it has proved itself over a long term. Farming, forestry and fishing employ a greater proportion of the work force here than in the Highlands as a whole, but no single occupation can provide a sure living for many individuals, who maintain themselves – usually to reasonable standards – by holding down seasonal or part-time jobs. A crofter may run his croft, a few cattle and sheep, assist in odd-jobbing and contracting, take on part-time forestry work, help to crew a local fishing boat, and so on, while his wife provides bed and breakfast for summer visitors. Here are a few basic employment figures, some of which, of course, vary with seasonal demands:

Agriculture   185
   (about half part-time, half self-employed)
Fishing   56
   (self-employed)

Forestry Commission	40
Forestry (private)	16
(including saw-milling)	
Services	180
(hotels, catering)	
Shops	100
Public service	200
(transport, education, health, local government, electricity, etc)	

The introduction of new light industries to Mull – for instance chocolate manufacturing at Dervaig – has been considered and tried out with limited success. There is the difficulty of staffing – unless in the future, under more normal industrial conditions throughout the country, the manpower that has always drifted away from Mull to the mainland can be induced to remain; and of course the millstones of transport costs and distance from markets are always there. In addition to these problems there is a lack of official interest and support at goverment level. We could learn many lessons from Norway in this connection.

At the same time the islanders are slow to venture into new local businesses, and it is found that the initiative to do so seems to lie with incomers. This may be partly due to lack of capital, but there may well be a hereditary reluctance to change from the old ways. However, as the expansion of the tourist industry indicates, Mull people are starting to take an interest in progress. Certainly the short season is a deterrent; but surely there could be some move to counter the imports of milk, fish, bread and vegetables. The launderette which opened in Tobermory in the late 1970s is a successful venture. Surely shoe repairing, barbering and so on – even on a part-time basis – could be established. Seventy years ago in a good season an apiary of six beehives produced several hundred-weights of the finest honey – which no-one would buy even at a price of sixpence (old currency) per pound section. Now, although it is a popular high-value foodstuff, Mull produces comparatively little.

THE SMALLER ISLANDS AND IONA

Properly speaking Mull is an island group consisting of the one large island and a number of much smaller ones on the western side. Chief among these are Staffa, Inch Kenneth, Ulva and Gometra, Erraid, Erisgeir, the Treshnish Islands, Eorsa, Little Colonsay and, of course, the sacred island of Iona. The economy, history and social problems of these islands are so closely interrelated with those of Mull itself that they form a comprehensive whole. The surface geology of all the islands, except Inch Kenneth, Iona and the southern islets, is similar to the volcanic basalts of western Mull.

ULVA AND GOMETRA

These are the largest of the islands, divided from the north-western promontory of Mull by the waters of Loch Tuath. Both are formed of basalt like the neighbouring part of the main island. Ulva (Wolf Island) is roughly 4½ miles from west to east and 2 miles from north to south; its basalt terraces rise to 1,025ft (312m) in its highest western portion. The coastline is very indented and has several striking basalt formations, and numerous off-shore rocks, reefs and islets. A raised beach, possibly of pre-glacial age, may be observed at about 150ft (45m) above sea-level on the southern shore between Tor Mor and A'Chrannag, and, at the back of this level, there is a huge sea cave, about a quarter of a mile inland from the present seashore.

A 'glen' deepened into a narrow sea channel, completely severs Gometra from the western end of Ulva. A bridge crosses the channel and carries the rough road from Ulva Ferry to Gometra House. Gometra, also with a very indented coastline and numerous off-shore reefs, is only 2 miles long and 1 mile wide. Although most of the surface is under 500ft (150m) in altitude, the island is rugged, with steep coasts. There is a private anchorage and quayside at the sheltered eastern end.

Ulva Ferry is a crossing of three hundred yards or so from the Torloisk shore of Mull. It is now a private ferry, but if the proprietor or the estate manager on Ulva, is given prior notice, arrangements will be made for the visitor who is genuinely interested to visit the island. This is to discourage casual sightseers who might well disturb valuable stock and spoil the amenities of this quiet island.

Both Ulva and Gometra have fertile, porous soil and a mild humid climate that combine to give a natural grassiness very well suited to cattle-grazing. However, the disturbance of the natural balance through the introduction of sheep last century led to the spread of rampant bracken growth, and the islands' potential resources are no longer fully utilised.

Ulva and Gometra were both densely populated. In 1843 some 800 people lived there, but five years later, hit first by the failure of the potato crop and immediately afterwards by the clearances and evictions, the population had fallen to 150 and was still falling. Now only a handful of estate workers live on the islands. The sheltered eastern side formerly produced splendid crops; some of the best potatoes in the Hebrides were grown in the rich basalt soil, with a surplus for export. Widespread ruins of old houses and settlements are a sad memorial to past prosperity.

The high, shadowed cliffs of Gribun stand boldly to the south across Loch na Keal. In sunny weather a long, bright triangle of sunshine falls through a cleft of the cliffs on to the lower slope. This, moving with the sun on the principle of a sundial, provided a rough measure of time for the people of Ulva in the days when clocks and watches were few or lacking.

Ulva was the clan territory of the MacQuarries; the chief of the clan who entertained Dr Johnson and Boswell lived to the age of 102.

The father of Maj-Gen Lachlan MacQuarie, Governor-General of New South Wales for ten or eleven years up to

1821, and known as the Father of Australia, was a small farmer on Ulva. As described earlier, the grandfather of the famous missionary and explorer Dr Livingstone was a crofter in the island before leaving for Glasgow and Blantyre. Ulva House, a modern mansion-house about half a mile from the ferry, replaces the building where Dr Johnson, Sir Walter Scott and other famous visitors were entertained. Part of the original house is built into the structure of the nearby factor's house.

INCH KENNETH

This fertile island has a level surface, rising to about 160ft (50m) at its highest, but is fringed by low broken cliffs. It measures about 1 mile by ½ mile and lies just south of the wide entrance to Loch na Keal, close under the great cliffs of Gribun. The proprietor runs a private ferry-boat between convenient landings on both sides of the channel. There is a fine nineteenth-century mansion-house on the island and an attractive bungalow-style farmhouse for the farmer who leases the land for crops and grazing.

Like Iona, the island differs in character from Mull, for the overlying lavas have been worn away to leave sedimentary rocks exposed that break down into a sandy soil capable of producing good crops. In early times the island was a veritable granary for the monks of Iona, like the more distant island of Tiree.

The island is named after Kenneth, a contemporary of St Columba, who is said to have saved him from drowning through the powers of prayer. Kenneth died abbot of Achabo, in Ireland, in AD600. In 1569 Inch Kenneth, with other concessions, belonged to the Prioress of Iona. In ecclesiastical importance it was second only to that island, and although no trace now remains of a monastery, there is a ruined chapel, measuring 40ft (12m) by 30ft (9m), the remains of a cross, and many old tombstones.

In 1773 Dr Johnson and Boswell were impressed by the '. . . pretty little island . . . all good land', where they were entertained, 'not by a gross herdsman or amphibious fisherman, but by a gentleman and two ladies of high birth, polished manners and elegant conversation, who in a habitation raised not far from the ground but furnished with unexpected neatness . . . practised all the kindness of hospitality and refinement of courtesy'.

Their hosts were Sir Alan Maclean (whose ornamental tombstone lies at the west end of the ruined chapel) and his two daughters. The low-roofed stone building where they were entertained is still in existence, though no longer used as a dwelling-house.

EORSA

This rugged island lies in the centre of Loch na Keal. Once frequented by wild goats along its western cliffs it is at present uninhabited, but supports a fair stock of sheep. At one time, like Inch Kenneth, it belonged to the Prioress of Iona. It served as a natural barrier across Loch na Keal during World War I, in particular for protecting the deep-water anchorage in Loch na Keal during occasional visits of the Grand Fleet, as well as being a rendezvous for Atlantic convoys.

STAFFA

Staffa lies well off the mouth of Loch na Keal, roughly halfway between the northern and southern promontories of western Mull. Its Norse name means 'Pillar Island' and graphically describes its striking formations of columnar basalt. A mile long by a quarter of a mile wide, it slopes gently upwards from the low northern shore to the bold cliffs along the south side which rise at one point to 135ft (40m) and are penetrated by a number of sea caves, some of which can be explored only by boat.

Best known is Fingal's Cave, which is 227ft (69m) deep, 66ft (20m) high and 42ft (13m) wide at the entrance. A path can be followed far into the cave along the tops of wave-cut basalt columns, which form a natural landing-stage in front. Its former Gaelic name meant 'Melodious Cave', and the usual flair of former inhabitants in adopting apt place names was confirmed when the echoing surge of the waves and the cries of sea-birds inspired the composition of Mendelssohn's overture that takes its name from the cave.

In the Clamshell Cave, which is 130ft (40m) deep, 30ft (9m) high and 18ft (5.5m) wide, the basalt columns, instead of being vertical, are angled or fantastically curved. The peculiar rock Buchaille (the Herdsman) is a conical pile of 30ft (9m) columns on a foundation of curved and horizontal pillars visible just off the Clamshell Cave. The Cormorant's (or MacKinnon's) Cave is 224ft (68m) deep, and the Boat Cave 150ft (45m) deep.

All these caves are at their most impressive under conditions of morning light. In stormy weather, all over the island the noise of breaking waves can be deafening. MacKinnon, Abbot of Iona (whose tomb lies beside the altar in the cathedral there), was so disturbed by the roar of the waves that he moved his cell from Staffa over to the vast quiet cave below Balmeanach Farm, Gribun, which now bears his name.

Staffa was unknown to the outside world until 1772 when the botanist Sir Joseph Banks, on board the *St Lawrence* on his way to Iceland, learned of the existence of Staffa and its wonders. Queen Victoria and Prince Albert landed on Staffa in 1847 and the Queen's impressions are recorded in her diary of the tour. For over a century now the island has been a centre of attraction for tourists and, together with Iona, it is visited every summer by tens of thousands.

The landing of sightseers from the then daily cruise ship from Oban was discontinued in 1968, partly because of the rising costs of the operation, partly because of the increasing danger of rock-falls in Fingal's Cave. The ship now lies close in to the island when weather permits, giving the opportunity to view and photograph the coastal formations. From Mull, however, motor cruisers now provide sightseeing trips off the west of Mull which include, by arrangement, a landing on Staffa.

As on so many of the other islands, the ruins of old habitations can be seen. The last families left Staffa in about 1800, leaving only the occasional herdsman to keep an eye on the livestock that used to be grazed there.

THE SMALLER ISLANDS AND IONA

This is no more than a rocky islet isolated in the seas west of the Ardmeanach promontory, a wide grassy rock on which a few sheep could be grazed. Because of its central position in the Mull group, Erisgeir figures prominently in a traditional story handed down from the fourteenth century. It is said that a chief of the clan Maclean, who up to then had had few connections with Mull, married Mary, daughter of the Lord of the Isles, whose wide possessions in the Hebrides included the island of Mull. In due course, when a child was born of the union, and when the Lord of the Isles promised a gift of land to his grandchild, the shrewd family nurse suggested that he should be asked to convey a grant of 'Little Erisgeir and her Isles'. To this the great chief of the MacDonalds thoughtlessly agreed, although he found to his chagrin that this included, among the isles, Mull itself. However, he kept to his word; and this, it is said, was the foundation of the subsequent power and possessions of the Clan Maclean.

TRESHNISH ISLES

This island group, strung out in a line north-east to south-east, lies 4–5 miles west of Gometra. They are the eroded marine remnants of a lava sheet. From north to south the main islands are: Cairnburg Beag (2 miles south-west of Treshnish Point), Cairnburg Mor, Fladda (Flat Island), Lunga (Long Island), Bac Mor and Bac Beag (the Great and Little Humps). Bac Mor is called the 'Dutchman's Cap' after its strange outline. In fact, observed from Loch na Keal and the north-west of Mull, these islands present arresting profiles, especially when seen standing out boldly against the unforgettable colours of a Hebridean sunset.

Landing is usually very difficult, partly because of the rocky shores, partly because of the fierce tides that run like a river between the reefs and islands. Facing the open Atlantic, they can be lashed by heavy seas and smothered in spray during stormy weather. Although now uninhabited, in the past they offered a convenient base for local fishermen and excellent grazings for cattle and sheep on the lush grass, where dew provided the moisture in place of surface water, which is lacking. The remains of two substantial houses can be seen on Lunga, to the north of the central hill (Cruachan, 337ft/103m) and above the shore where the rough pebbly beach provides a precarious landing-place sheltered by the neighbouring islet, Sgeir a'Chaisteal, with its contorted rocky outline.

A walk of fifteen minutes along the top of the 100ft (30m) cliff takes the visitor to Dun Cruit – the Harp Rock – so called through the resemblance of its silhouette to a Celtic harp. It is a portion of the cliff isolated by an angled chasm where the sea surges wildly 100ft (30m) below. The grassy summit of the formation has been worn away by the nesting habits of burrowing puffins. Roughly in the centre of Lunga there is a cave leading from a hollow to the seashore, with rough steps leading down into it; undoubtedly a place used by man in the distant past. (The Cairnburgs have been fully described under 'Castles'.)

The Treshnish Islands are a sanctuary for sea-birds and a breeding-place for a colony of grey seals. Autumn is the best time to study the seals while May and early June are the best time to watch the sea-birds, the islands are crowded with nesting birds or their young – puffins, cormorants, shag, gulls of many varieties, and other species. Their clamours of protest can be deafening at the approach of a stranger. In former days young sea-birds and their eggs were an important food item. Fishermen used to carry the mast of a skiff along to the Harp Rock, lower it across the chasm, and crawl across to collect the eggs and the young – especially those of the puffin, which were salted down in barrels for winter consumption – which they carried back across the chasm in bags made of old nets. In spite of this hair-raising crossing only one mishap is said to have taken place when the man slipped and vanished down into the boiling surf below. The very few shallow pools of surface water are heavily fouled by sea-birds.

The 'brim' of the Dutchman's Cap is an eroded lava platform; the 'crown' is capped by the remnant of an overlying flow.

A cruise to these islands should not be missed.

THE SMALLER ISLANDS AND IONA

This island, roughly a mile square, lies close to the south-west tip of the Ross of Mull. It is accessible dry-shod at low tide. Until recent years it was a shore station for keepers of the lighthouses at Skerryvore and Dhuheartach which stand 24 and 15 miles distant respectively, on their dangerous submerged reefs in the open sea. The station was abandoned in 1967 and the houses sold by the Commissioners of Northern Lights. This is the inhospitable island that Robert Louis Stevenson described so vividly in *Kidnapped*, on which David Balfour, after being confined on the brig *Covenant*, was cast away and began his adventurous flight through the heather. It is little wonder that Stevenson described the background so well, for he had lived there and explored the district during the time his uncle, Alan Stevenson, was engineering the building of the two lighthouses mentioned, as well as Ardnamurchan lighthouse, and certain piers and jetties, all of which were built mostly of the Ross of Mull granite. Skerryvore, completed in 1844, was the tallest lighthouse around the coasts of Britain until the building of Eddystone in 1882.

Three miles south of Erraid lie the Torran (Thunder) rocks, so-called on account of the roar of the Atlantic waves breaking over them in stormy weather. This is a wild and dangerous coast given a wide berth by shipping. Stevenson's *The Merry Men* also relates to the coast around Erraid.

FRANK LOCKWOOD'S ISLAND

This is just a tiny island lying off the mouth of Lochbuie. Its interest lies in a sentimental name that is unique in an area of almost exclusively Gaelic or Norse place names.

Frank Lockwood, who rose to be Sir Frank Lockwood, QC, and Solicitor-General in Lord Rosebery's administration of 1894–5, was the brother-in-law of Murdoch Gillean, 21st MacLaine of Lochbuie. MacLaine married Catherine, youngest daughter of Salis Schwabe of Anglesey, while Lockwood married her sister Julia in 1874.

IONA

A great deal has been written about Iona. Indeed its significance is such that it warrants full treatment in a separate book and what follows is no more than a brief general summary. It is now a busy sunny holiday island in summer, with bays of dazzling white sand and green translucent water in the mile-wide Sound of Iona that separates it from Mull on its eastern side. There are fine views from Iona towards the massive mountains of central Mull which not only protect it from the worst of the east winds but also attract the westerly rain clouds upwards before they have had time to precipitate their heaviest rains on the little island.

Three miles from north to south and one and a half from east to west, Iona is about 2,000 acres (800ha) in extent, rising at its highest point to 332ft (101m) at Dun-i. Its shores are washed by the relatively warm waters of the North Atlantic Drift and its climate is even more equable than that of Mull. It is composed mainly of ancient Lewisian gneiss, in contrast with its larger neighbour. What were once bands of limestone in this rock have been recrystallised by heat and pressure and converted into marble, for which Iona is famous. The island is sandy and fertile. A third of its area is cultivated and the rest is grazing and rocky bogland.

The present permanent population is about sixty, mostly centred in the little village near the Abbey, connected by ferry with Fionnphort, the Mull terminus, across the Sound. The population stood at 500 in 1842, but, as in surrounding districts, fell rapidly thereafter. In summer, accommodation is strained to the limit to meet the holiday requirements of hundreds of visitors. Fresh water used to be in limited supply but the shortage has been overcome by the construction of a small reservoir on the south-west side of the island. In early days a small burn, large enough to turn a little corn-mill, flowed near the village, with a shallow dam (or fish-pond) beside the abbey garden. Few traces of this remain. With under 3 miles of passable roads, only a few essential vehicles are found on Iona.

Iona, the island of Saint Columba, is steeped in history and tradition. Here we can 'See the moon on royal tombstones gleam' and read in carved coats of arms the story of men who lived, preached, fought and died, back to the dawn of Christianity in Scotland. The atmosphere is well conveyed by Dr Johnson's words: 'We are now treading that illustrious Island, which was once the luminary of the Caledonian regions, whence savage clans and roving barbarians derived the benefits of knowledge and the blessings of religion . . . That man is little to be envied whose . . . piety would not grow warmer among the ruins of Iona.'

The magnificence of Iona began in AD563 when Columba, with his twelve disciples, landed on the southern tip of the island at Port na Churaich (the Harbour of the Coracle). The coracles of those days were sometimes quite large craft, built of wickerwork over a frame of wooden strengtheners, then covered with hides and well caulked. The Woodrow manuscript, dated 1701, which is kept in the Advocates' Library, Edinburgh, records that the coracle of St Columba measured 60ft (18m) in length, being the distance between two stone pillars set up on the shore as markers and still visible there. On the shore, too, are to be seen piles of stones said to have been raised as penances by the monks; as Pennant wrote rather pawkily, 'To judge by some of these heaps it is no breach of charity to think there were among them enormous sinners.'

Columba was a prince of Ireland, grandson of Niall of the Nine Hostages and High King of Ireland, and in religion, to which he devoted his life, he was a follower of St Patrick. He came to Scotland as a salve to his conscience and voluntary banishment as a penance after a well-meaning but ill-judged action which had led to great bloodshed. Hearing that a colleague, the abbot Fenian, had returned from Rome with a new and simplified translation of the Gospels, Columba sought to obtain a copy, but was refused. Secretly borrowing the script, he was discovered when completing a copy of it. He refused to return or destroy his private notes, even when ordered to do so by the High King of Ireland, before whom the dispute was brought, and who pronounced the famous

THE SMALLER ISLANDS AND IONA

verdict on copyright: 'To every cow its calf, and to every book its copy.'

Columba was adamant. Both factions took up arms, the traditionalist and the seeker after a simpler approach. There followed a battle, with great loss of life; and although Columba emerged the winner, he was so overcome with remorse that as a penance he decided to leave Ireland for ever and settle where he could never again see the hills of his native land.

This dedication to simplicity led Columba to found the Celtic Church, or the Church of the Culdees (meaning Servants of God). The Culdees spread the doctrine of St Columba, following his principles of clear interpretation in the language of his listeners, right across Scotland. Under the floor of the splended Norman nave of Dunfermline Abbey, Fife, parts of the foundations of an early church of the Culdees can be seen, showing that the Culdees must have been active at least up to the tenth and eleventh centuries. The tenets of St Columba's church were never wholly approved by the parent Church of Rome, which later effectively ended the influence of the Culdees and restored the traditional orthodoxy of the parent church.

St Columba was by no means the first missionary to come over from Ireland. St Ninian, St Bride, St Maolruabh (the Red Saint of Applecross) and others were before him; but while their influence was local, this 'Morning Star of Scotland's Faith' brought with him from Ireland the traditions of the Celtic Christian church, establishing in Iona a school of learning – the 'University of the North', as it came to be called – that attracted scholars and pilgrims, and the practice of writing, that during the next century, through the evangelism of monks, was to influence not only Dalriadic Scots on the neighbouring mainland, but also the Picts and Northumbrians, and even to reach beyond their lands, far into the continent of Europe, and to Scandinavia through the Vikings. This Celtic culture, centring on Ireland and Iona, came next in antiquity to that of Greece and Rome.

In the seventh century the monks built an abbey church which was subsequently pillaged by the invading Norsemen in search of the gold and other treasures that could usually be found in Irish churches. Between 794 and 986 the island was pillaged six times. After 1069 the abbey church was restored and in about 1200 a Benedictine Monastary and a convent of the Black Nuns were established nearby. The convent is now a picturesque ruin from every chink of whose stonework flowers grow in profusion. In spite of the resurgence, the great days of the island as a source of Christian teaching were long past, and three centuries later Iona was turned into a sacred desert more systematically and finally than had been achieved by earlier pagan ravages. In 1561 an Act was passed at the desire of the Reformed Church in Scotland 'for demolishing all the abbeys of monks and friars, and for suppressing whatsoever monuments of idolatrie were remaining in the realm'. Armed with this authority the fanatical Reformers ruthlessly destroyed the learning of ages, records of the Scottish and Irish nations, beautiful archives of remote antiquity, and revered and lovely buildings. Of the 360 crosses said to have been standing in Iona, only three can now be seen. Many of the books and records were carried away by the fleeing monks. Some still lie in the Vatican, others in Switzerland and elsewhere. A few – very few – remain in our own museums. Hearsay has it that some such relics were hidden in the fortress-island of Cairnburg Mor, but were retrieved and destroyed by Cromwell and the Covenanters.

Iona belonged to the Macleans of Duart until it passed into the hands of the Duke of Argyll. Restoration began in a small way in 1899, when the eighth Duke made over the abbey buildings to the Church of Scotland for the use of all Christian denominations, in the hope that it might be rebuilt. This has now been done by the dedicated work of the Iona Community, a body of voluntary workers founded in 1938 under the inspired guidance of Rev George MacLeod, now Lord MacLeod of Fiunary.

In the reconstruction by the Iona Community, one can trace much of the original structure, for which most of the red granite must have been rafted across the Sound of Iona from the Tormore quarries by the eleventh-century builders. The monk architects and masons painstakingly hammered and chipped the walls to a plain surface. They were not without an impish sense of humour, to judge by some of the original whimsical and symbolic carvings around the tops of arches and pillars a quality found too in the carvings on the stonework of Notre Dame, in Paris, and elsewhere. They are grotesque carvings which were supposed to repel the influence of evil spirits, a lingering superstition. A permanent light, marked on Admiralty charts, is in the St Columba shrine, adjacent to the west door of the Abbey.

An old Mull tradition has it that St Columba would allow neither women nor cattle to live on Iona during his lifetime, and there is a Gaelic saying attributed to him that is still current in the islands:

> Far am bi bò bithidh bean;
> Is far am bi bean bithidh molluchadh!

> (Where there is a cow there is a woman;
> And where there is a woman there's mischief!)

The women were banished over to Eilean nam Ban (Women's Island), the rocky island which lies below the Tormore quarries and shelters the ruined jetty and the anchorage in the bay, known to yachters as the Bullhole; ancient ruins are still visible on the island. The ban was relaxed after the death of Columba and by 1203 the convent of the Black Nuns had been founded by the MacDonalds.

Iona became a place of interment for great men from far places. Forty-eight Scottish kings lie there, from Fergus II to MacBeth, as well as kings from Norway and France, clan chiefs and dignitaries and holy men associated with the monastery. According to tradition (for there is no record of this) an Archbishop of Canterbury is buried there, and a Norwegian princess, interred with a treasure of gold around her.

There were two reasons for the desirability of Iona as a last resting place. One was the comforting thought of lying for all time in such holy ground. The other was more subtle and secular – the wish to lie for all time in an island of lasting permanence. It is remarkable how the unscientific people of those early days seemed to be instinctively aware of the geological antiquity and permanence of Iona as an island. A very old Gaelic prophecy translated and paraphrased long ago by Dr Smith of Campbeltown illustrates this:

> Seven years before that awful day
> When time shall be no more
> A watery deluge will o'ersweep
> Hibernia's mossy shore.
>
> The green-clad Isla, too, shall sink
> While with the great and good
> Columba's happy isle will rear
> Her towers above the flood.

The sanctity that Columba brought to Iona seems still to be present there and it is striking how easily the gap of 1,400 years seems to be bridged. St Columba might have lived there no more than a century ago. His sayings are common in Mull and Iona, as are stories of his life, traditions and accounts of the miracles attributed to him. Places where he preached are still pointed out; indeed, at Salen, at the Rock, his congregation is reputed to have been rather scanty!

13   *A VIEW OF THE FUTURE*

For one of Mull parentage and brought up on the island, it is with mixed feelings that one has become aware of the slow changes that have taken place in its economy. The solid traditional basis of agriculture has been eroded both by social changes and by the spread of plantations that sterilise grazing lands and are turning the roads into green tunnels. Tiny but once thriving crofts are desolate, bracken-infested, or with a handful of sheep grazing on what is left of the grasslands. Labour costs are high, capital is in short supply and living is expensive on an island. Can it be wondered at that job opportunities are comparatively few and young people naturally drift away to seek employment on the mainland, leaving an ageing population to carry on?

True, at the time of writing this population drift has halted, and has even been reversed, although this may be a temporary phase brought about by lack of work on the mainland, for during a period of depression and unemployment, there is no inducement to leave the island.

However, the picture is not all black. While agriculture has declined, a prosperous new industry is developing – the tourist trade – and as figures quoted earlier in this book bear out, this is taking a vital place in the economy of Mull. Unfortunately, it is a precarious industry, dependent on factors outside the control of the islanders. Meanwhile, Mull is very much on the map and has become a popular holiday island and one which attracts retired people tired of the exacting demands of modern life in urban and industrial areas. It is good to see ruined houses restored, new houses built and public utilities extended.

Many small family ventures have come into being to cater for tourist demands, from the running of small cruise boats to pony-trekking and angling, as well as excellent craft shops producing quality goods. However, one significant fact is that such little businesses are usually initiated by newcomers to the island; whether this is due to lack of capital, or of specialised skills, or slowness to adapt to change, on the part of the indigenous Mull people is hard to say. Unfortunately, no real impact has been made by light industries, although the facilities are there. Always there is the deterrent of heavy overhead costs, even if the capital is there for investment. Without some drastic and constructive approach to the question at government level, light industries will be hesitant about coming to the island.

Much of the blame for the unimaginative approach to Mull's economy lies fairly and squarely on the policy of successive governments too obsessed by the problems of industry generally, and too anxious to appease the big battalions, to give more than cursory consideration to the Highlands and Islands. The policy appears to be a system of social security, doles, grants and subsidies sufficient to keep the people quiet and the economy ticking over. No effective fact-finding commission has been appointed; no practical comparison made with such similar areas in Norway, the Faeroes and Iceland. (The Scottish Tourist Board even has to be represented abroad by the British Tourist Board. Surely Scotland in general and the Hebridean islands in particular can offer enough to justify a flourishing and independent board of its own.)

The financial benefits of subsidies in their present form are offset by the heavy transport costs of monopolistic communications services. How much better, for example, to subsidise the cost of petrol by equating the price to that on the nearest point of the mainland; to reconsider and introduce the Roads Equivalent Tariff, which at one stroke would reduce the 20 per cent higher living costs in the island, besides revitalising all freight movements, and end some of the futureless subsidies.

Serious consideration will have to be given to Mull's increasingly congested side-roads, for the safety and pleasure of visitors to the island, as well as for the benefit of local traffic

211

movements. The side-roads still follow the lines used in the days of the horse and cart, with narrow bridges, unbottomed sections over boglands, subsiding culverts, gradients and blind corners. These roads will simply collapse when massive loads of timber begin to move with the felling of mature timber in the north of Mull. Again, for a country that ploughs back into road maintenance only one-tenth of the revenue obtained from vehicular traffic, a new approach should be made to the problems of out-of-date roads in Mull and everywhere else, even simply for the sake of providing much-needed employment.

While Mull, with its affinities to the Highland Region, is on the perimeter of the top-heavy Strathclyde Region, it has not been neglected, and the Argyll and Bute District Council, which is responsible for so many of the services, has helped within the framework of its finances. The future of Mull lies beyond that, in the central government, which should take a genuine and constructive interest in the 'quiet failure of the simple people to obtain subsistence from their environment'.

BIBLIOGRAPHY

Most of the literature about Mull was published before World War I or immediately afterwards. Little was conveyed in it of the permanent changes in the way of life of the islanders over the last two centuries. More recent material than this is most frequently in the socio-economic and historical fields and occurs in books and articles that in general cover a much wider region than the island, or even Argyll – usually the Highlands and Islands of Scotland.

The earliest to write about the island were without exception travellers – explorers would be a better description – from the Lowlands of Scotland and from England. Not all accounts were flattering, which was hardly surprising in view of the tedium and austerity of contemporary travel.

Probably the very earliest was the tenth-century Dean of Lismore. Sir Donald Munro, High Dean of the Isles, travelled extensively throughout the Western Isles. In 1549 he produced his *Genealogies of the Chieff Clans of the Isles*, in which Mull and its inhabitants are described. This and other descriptive writings of his were published in 1773–4 as *Description of the Western Isles of Scotland called Hybrides* and a second volume, *Miscellanea Scotia*. Copies of the manuscripts are preserved in the Advocates' Library in Edinburgh.

In 1702 Sacheverell, Governor of the Isle of Man, published a report on his excursion through Mull in 1688, when early salvage operations were being attempted on the sunken galleon of the Armada fleet in Tobermory Bay. It has not been possible to trace the title or whereabouts of this report, but a quotation from it by MacCormick in 1923 describes the dress, armour and general appearance of the people of Mull with a certain admiration and respect.

Martin Martin, one of the Martins of Duntuilm in Skye, was hired as literary tutor for the MacLeods of Dunvegan. He was a most observant man who travelled extensively in the Western Isles and published a short paper in 1697 which was more formally presented in London in 1703 under the title *A Description of the Western Islands of Scotland*.

213

BIBLIOGRAPHY

Thomas Pennant's *A Tour in Scotland and Voyage to the Hebrides*, published in 1772, is well known. It describes his journey of 1769 when he had 'the hardihood to venture on a journey to the remotest part of North Britain', of which he brought home an account so favourable that 'it has ever since been *mondée* with Southern visitors'. His research into local history and traditions makes fascinating reading.

Among the tourists of the eighteenth century who visited Mull were Dr Samuel Johnson and Boswell, both of whom described their island journey of 1773, respectively in *Journey to the Western Islands* and *Journal of a Tour to the Hebrides with Samuel Johnson*.

In 1772 Sir Joseph Banks first described the marvels of Staffa and Fingal's Cave; his description was inserted in Pennant's *Tour*. John McCulloch, geologist and scientist, published among other papers *A Description of the Western Islands of Scotland* (1819) and *Highlands and Western Isles of Scotland* (1824).

James Hogg and even the poet Keats were here; descriptions of Mull or references to it have come into the writings of Thomas Campbell, Robert Louis Stevenson, Sir Walter Scott and others who drew on their experience there. Even Queen Victoria's diary has a reference to the island (*Leaves from my Journal* describes her visit to Staffa in 1847).

Argyll, Duke of. 'On Tertiary leaf-beds in the Isle of Mull', *Quarterly Journal of the Geological Society*, vii (1851), 89–103

Bailey, E. B. *Tertiary and post-Tertiary Geology of Mull, Lochaline and Oban* (1924)

Baker, Richard. *The Terror of Tobermory* (W. H. Allen, 1972)

Cregeen, Eric R. (ed) *Argyll Estate Instructions (Mull, Morvern and Tiree) 1771–1805* (Edinburgh, 1964)

Darling, F. Fraser. *A Herd of Red Deer* (Oxford, 1937)

—— (ed) *West Highland Survey: An Essay in Human Ecology* (Oxford, 1955)

—— and Boyd, J. Morton. *The Highlands and Islands* (1964) (A revised and rewritten version of F. Fraser Darling, *Natural History in the Highlands and Islands*, 1947)

Duckworth, C. L. D. and Langmuir, G. E. *West Highland Steamers* (Prescot, 1967)

Ellis, M. H. *Lachlan Macquarie: His Life, Adventures and Times* (1958)

Ewing, P. 'Contribution to the Topographical botany of the West of Scotland', *Proceedings and Transactions*, Natural History Society of Glasgow, New Series III (1892)

Gerrans, M. B. 'Notes on the flora of the Isle of Mull', *Proceedings of the Botanical Society of the British Isles*, 3 (1960), 369–74

Glover, Janet R. *The Story of Scotland* (1960)

Gordon, Seton. *Highways and Byways in the West Highlands* (1935)
—— *The Land of the Hills and the Glens* (1920)

Graham, H. D. *The Birds of Iona and Mull* (Edinburgh, 1890)

Graham, H. G. *The Social Life of Scotland in the Eighteenth Century* (1906, 1937)

Grant, I. F. *Economic History of Great Britain* (1934)
—— *Highland Folk Ways* (1961)

Gunn, Neil. *Off in a Boat* (1938)

Hannan, Thomas. *The Beautiful Isle of Mull* (Edinburgh, 1926)

Harker, Alfred. *The West Highlands and Hebrides* (Cambridge, 1941)

Jermy, A. C. and Crabbe, J. A. (eds) *The Isle of Mull: A Survey of its Flora and Environment* (British Museum (Natural History), 1978)

Johnston, W. J. *History of the Celtic Place Names of Scotland* (Edinburgh, 1926)

Johnston, Thomas. *Our Scots Noble Families* (Forward Publishing, Glasgow, 1913)

MacClure, V. *Scotland's Inner Man* (1935)

MacCormick, John. *The Island of Mull: its History, Scenes and Legends* (Glasgow 1923)

MacColla, Fionn. *The Albanach* (Souvenir Press, 1984)

MacDonald, James. *General View of the Agriculture of the Hebrides* (Edinburgh 1811)

MacKenzie, Osgood. *A Hundred Years in the Highlands* (1949)

Maclean, J. P. *History of the Isle of Mull* (2 vols) (Frank H. Jobes & Son, Printers, Ohio, 1923)

MacLeod, R. C. *The MacLeods of Dunvegan* (Clan MacLeod Society publication for members, Edinburgh, 1927)

Macnab, P. A. *Tall Tales from an Island (and other stories)* (Luath Press Ltd, Barr, Ayrshire, 1984)

Menzies, Lucy. *St Columba of Iona* (Edinburgh, 1935)

Munro, Neil. *Para Handy and other Tales* (Edinburgh and London, 1923)
—— *The Lost Pibroch* (Blackwood, 1923)

O'Dell, A. C. and Walton, K. *The Highlands and Islands of Scotland* (1962)

Piggott, Stuart (ed). *The Prehistoric Peoples of Scotland* (1962)

Plant, Marjorie. *Domestic Life of Scotland in the Eighteenth Century* (Edinburgh, 1952)

Pryde, G. S. *Scotland from 1603 to the Present Day* (1962)

BIBLIOGRAPHY

Rainsford-Hannay, F. *Drystone Walling* (1957)

Richey, J. E. *British Regional Geology, Scotland: The Tertiary Volcanic Districts* (1964)

Ritchie, T. *Iona Past and Present* (Highland Home Industries Ltd, Edinburgh, 1945)

Ross, G. 'On the Flora of Mull', *Transactions*, Botanical Society, Edinburgh, XIII 1878

Skene, W. F. *Celtic Scotland*, vol III (Edinburgh, 1880)

Small, A. 'Historical Geography of the Norse and Viking Colonisations of the Scottish Highlands,' *Norsk Geografisk Tidsskrift*, 22 (1968)

Thom, A. *Megalithic Sites in Britain* (Oxford, 1968)

Thomson, D. C. and Grimble, I. *The Future of the Highlands* (1968)

Wilmott, A. J. 'Report on the excursion to the Isle of Mull July–August 1939', *Report* for 1939–40, The Botanical Society and Exchange Club, 12 (1942)

Argyll & Bute District Council. *Mull, Coll and Tiree Local Plan* (May 1984)

Argyll County Council. *Mull: A Study in Rural Planning* (1965)

Court Proceedings of Royal Commission, (Highlands and Islands), official report. (1892)

Royal Commission on the Ancient and Historical Monuments of Scotland. *Argyll: An Inventory of the Monuments*, vol 3 (1980)

Royal Society of Edinburgh. *Proceedings: Selected Papers*, Vol 83, Sect. B (1983)

Society of Antiquarians of Scotland. *Proceedings* 1914–15 to 1946–47

The Statistical Account of Scotland, vols II and III (Edinburgh, 1791–9); *The New Statistical Account of Scotland*, vol VII (Edinburgh, 1845); *Third Statistical Account of Scotland*, vol IX, *County of Argyll* (Edinburgh, 1961)

MAPS

The current 1in Ordnance Survey maps covering Mull are sheets 47, 48 and 49 (1:50,000); Bartholomew's Contoured Maps of Great Britain No 47 (Mull and Oban) (1:100,000) which includes Mull and all its islands. Sheets 43 and 44 of the Geological Survey 1in maps cover western Mull and central and eastern Mull respectively.

ACKNOWLEDGEMENTS

It would be wearisome for readers and embarrassing for individuals to give the names of the many people whose valuable help and interest contributed to the preparation of this book. I thank the following for their patience in answering my queries and the useful technical information they supplied:

Campbell K. Finlay, of the former Mull and Iona Council of Social Service; the County Clerk of the former Argyll County Council; the Town Clerk of the former Burgh of Tobermory; the Director-General, Meteorological Office; the Forestry Commission, Scotland; the Public Relations Officer, British Telecom (Scotland West); John Hopkins & Co Ltd, Glasgow; Argyll and Bute District Council, Lochgilphead and Tobermory; the Chief Librarians, Ayr, and the Mitchell Library, Glasgow; the North of Scotland Hydro-Electric Board; Caledonian MacBrayne Ltd; the Department of Agriculture and Fisheries for Scotland (Economics and Statistics Unit); the Head Postmaster, Oban; David Guthrie James, of Torosay; the Highlands and Islands Development Board; West of Scotland College of Agriculture, Oban; Dr E. M. Patterson; Major J. R. E. Nelson, Glengorm.

INDEX

Page numbers in italic indicate illustrations

219

INDEX

INDEX

INDEX